CW00797486

# SO THIS IS PERMANENCE

*also by Deborah Curtis*

TOUCHING FROM A DISTANCE:
Ian Curtis and Joy Division

*also by Jon Savage*

ENGLAND'S DREAMING:
The Sex Pistols and Punk Rock

THE FABER BOOK OF POP:
edited with Hanif Kureishi

TEENAGE:
The Creation of Youth 1875–1945

# SO THIS IS PERMANENCE

---

## IAN CURTIS

EDITED BY DEBORAH CURTIS
& JON SAVAGE

JOY DIVISION
LYRICS AND NOTEBOOKS

FABER & FABER

First published in 2014
by Faber & Faber Ltd
Bloomsbury House, 74–77 Great Russell Street,
London WC1B 3DA
This paperback edition first published in 2015

Typeset by Faber & Faber Ltd
Printed in China

All rights reserved

Lyrics © Fractured Music / Universal Music Publishing
Foreword © Deborah Curtis, 2014
Introduction © Jon Savage, 2014

The right of Ian Curtis to be identified as author of this work
has been asserted in accordance with Section 77 of the Copyright,
Designs and Patents Act 1988

The right of Deborah Curtis and Jon Savage to be identified as editors
of this work has been asserted in accordance with Section 77 of the
Copyright, Designs and Patents Act 1988

A CIP record for this book
is available from the British Library

ISBN 978–0–571–30957–3

2 4 6 8 10 9 7 5 3 1

# CONTENTS

Foreword                                                      vii

Introduction                                                  xiii

Editorial Note                                                xxix

THE HANDWRITTEN LYRICS                                        1

APPENDIX ONE                                                  105
Early versions, alternatives, new songs, prose

APPENDIX TWO                                                  219
Artwork, fanzines, books, letters

Acknowledgements                                             273

# FOREWORD
# BY DEBORAH CURTIS

I was introduced to Ian in Macclesfield in 1972 by a boy he called his brother. This singular teenager, who didn't go to the youth club with the other kids, stood posing on the balcony of his parents' flat. He was wearing eye makeup, tight jeans and a fun fur jacket; some would have laughed but there was a reverence about that first encounter. He appeared to be waiting for the introduction. It felt preordained.

He was studious: winning a school History prize in 1971 and the Divinity prize in 1971 and 1972, enjoying Ted Hughes and Thom Gunn and later Chaucer. He had a black ring binder with subject dividers which he had marked 'Lyrics' and 'Novel', and I felt privileged that he had trusted me enough to let me see the extent of his ambitions.

I was hooked; the romance of him being both a poet and a writer was too much to resist; and it was easy to settle into the lifestyle of being around him. He took me to gigs, introduced me to the diverse people in his life and when I realised that our future was to be together nothing else seemed to matter.

Apart from his vinyl collection and reams of music papers his bedroom was impersonal, especially considering his complex theatrical personality. There were no piles of clothes or makeup or clutter of any kind. He was tidy and cared obsessively how things looked and sounded, always striving for perfection. He juggled his relationships easily, moving between different peer groups, collecting other people and their experiences.

He approached difficult subjects so obliquely that I couldn't detect whether they were pertinent to him personally. I didn't understand why he wanted to talk about a local boy who was said to be suffering from manic depression; it seemed like gossip and was uncharacteristic of him. He explained any of his own unusual behaviour, absences or seizures as 'flashbacks' and it was made clear that they were not up for discussion.

There were rumours that Ian had been in trouble at school but his friends laughed, the Curtis family moved to Manchester and it was all brushed away. Their front lounge became his bedroom; again it was tidy and functional, all he seemed to need in life were his records, the music press and cigarettes.

When I stayed at the weekend he would put on a record and we would sit on the floor. Each album had to be listened to from beginning to end uninterrupted and he loved explaining the story behind the lyrics to me. He liked to read Oscar Wilde or Edgar Allan Poe and he would make sure we were home on Saturday nights in time to watch the horror films.

We married and for a while we lived with his grandparents. Ian began buying reggae music; he would wait until we were alone before he carried his record player into the lounge, the thick net curtains and the heavy drapes blocking the daylight. Ian no longer had a room of his own but he didn't put a hold on his plans.

Ian liked to call into the record shop in Moss Side shopping centre to listen to the latest releases and from there he found out where the best reggae clubs were. We went to The Mayflower and The Afrique and got out of the house as much as possible. He saw it as an opportunity to meet the people who lived in that area, to immerse himself in another culture. We soaked up the atmosphere in the local shops and went out in the evenings to collect the money for the football coupons. No matter how late we were out the night before, Ian would insist that we were up and in work by 8 a.m. so we could finish early and go out again.

Our first home was in Chadderton where it was quiet, inconvenient for nights out in Manchester and far away from our friends in Macclesfield. Our lounge was the only room that was heated and comfortable, but somehow, even without the necessary privacy, Ian began to write again, keeping his work in a plastic carrier bag. It was from that address that we set off for the Mont-de-Marsan Punk Rock Festival; after that trip our world opened up and everything felt possible.

We put the house on the market knowing only that we weren't happy there. After a short stint back at his grandparents' we moved to Macclesfield. The house on Barton Street was double-fronted, with a kitchen and lounge on one side of the staircase and another completely separate room on the other.

I saw a beautiful, cosy cottage within walking distance of the town centre but Ian saw a room all of his own: a space to write, small enough for the electric fire to heat and long enough for him to pace up and down with his thoughts. We couldn't wait to move in and the first task was to make Ian's room ready: he painted it sky blue, and we acquired a radiogram. Ian's plastic carrier bag had its place on the blue carpet next to the long blue Habitat sofa, and his albums leaned stacked against the wall behind the door.

It didn't cross my mind that one of the shared rooms should be first on the agenda for refurbishment: Ian's writing career was paramount for both of us. He would move the ashtray from the floor to the top of the wooden fire surround depending on whether he was pacing or sitting. He was a neat smoker, never allowing ash to accumulate; often the only sound would be the click of his long thumbnail on the filter tip of his Marlboro before he balanced it on the edge of his ashtray to pick up his pen. He would write a line, put the pen down and then knock more ash from his cigarette.

He took the carrier bag with him to rehearsals, on tour, and to meetings. When he came home he would stand on the doorstep, pushing the door open as he turned the key; the bag rustling noisily as he fumbled was always the first sound I heard; then straight to the blue room to stow his writing away before he took off his coat and hung it in the cupboard. There was never anything superfluous in his life as he chose his surroundings as carefully as he chose his words.

Ian's art was crucial to him and he did not consider songwriting a mere commercial endeavour. So it was unsurprising that he turned to darker, more serious subjects to inspire him. Not specifically the Holocaust but war itself: any war would have been the perfect vehicle for Ian's interpretation of the world. In conversation he would touch vaguely on his Irish family history and on his father's subsequent service in World War II. It's debatable whether he drew on those stories to fuel his creative process or whether he turned to writing because speaking out was frowned upon.

Ian was compassionate, empathetic and kind, never ostentatious or materialistic. His ability to fully immerse himself in the thread of another life was easily demonstrated when he read to me, whether it was lyrics or prose, and that passion continued into his stage presence. At first his performance served well to deflect attention away from his inner self and it was amazing to see someone normally so taciturn become so dynamically animated in performance.

He didn't show me his work and I was shy about asking to see it. I can remember once taking a peek and tentatively (he didn't take criticism well) suggesting that a word be changed. To my surprise he did this without argument, but later in his career I had more of a sense of his notes being out of bounds.

He was away so regularly that his role in Joy Division became more like a job than the fulfilment it was meant to be. When the band performed 'Digital' and 'Glass' at the Russell Club (renamed the Factory for the event) it was a pivotal moment for us; I was both proud and scared. I hadn't heard those songs before: the set was so polished, the music had matured and the audience went wild. I felt myself shrink to the back of the room as if I had stumbled upon a secret. Their genius had hardly been accomplished overnight but it was still shocking to see this evidence of how hard they'd been working.

Ian's brainstorming notes refer to corruption, politics, government, and sociological issues: he continually searched for influences, situations he could put himself in. He had always been professional and driven but as his dream became his reality, his lyrics began to talk of impossible choices and ineffective treatment.

Ian was diagnosed with epilepsy whilst I was pregnant. His family refused point blank to discuss it. I don't even know if that was the first time he had been given a diagnosis; yet when the doctors repeatedly asked if he'd had fits before, I was complicit and joined with him in a resounding, 'No.' Ian used his epilepsy as a barrier and focused his work on feelings of isolation, loss and spectacle.

I felt he wanted to talk to me, but he became resentful at home as if broaching the subject of his illness aloud made it more real. However, as the gap between us widened and filled up with complicated secrets, he continued to exhibit his frustration and pain in front of an audience. His writing didn't so much develop as ripen, so much so that you can hear the bruising in his voice.

How did I feel when I was told by Rob Gretton that 'Love Will Tear Us Apart' was about me? Angry, humiliated; I scoured his manuscripts looking for evidence that it wasn't so. *Your bedroom, this bedroom, the bedroom*: he played with these variations. Was he trying to depersonalise the lyrics or did he genuinely not know which bedroom he was referring to? Of course, now I can see that it was another situation he could draw on and not that different to writing about a tragedy he might see on the news; but the burden of finding a way to displace what was happening in his life must have twisted him to the core.

When I read the lyrics now I hear the music in my head, I hear his voice, I see him. A manuscript with crossings-out and corrections conjures an image of him in the blue room, pacing and smoking, barely noticing when I handed a cup of coffee into the room.

Some of the lyrics can be dated by what they're written on: scrap paper taken from the office where I was working, a sheet taken from a journalist's notepad when I was at college, possible album titles scrawled in blue ballpoint over lightly pencilled Pitman shorthand, and many on the now redundant foolscap-size paper. Several folded pages have clearly been stuffed in his pocket for some time before they were written on; even without the carrier bag he liked to make sure he was equipped should the right words come to him.

When New Order wanted to record 'Ceremony' and 'In a Lonely Place' they asked to see all Ian's notes because they were convinced that the lyrics to those songs would still be with the rest of his work. They studied them intently but the relevant lyrics were not there. This isn't strange; Ian would dispose of things he no longer needed; he could be very unsentimental about his belongings and from what he told me he considered his work with Joy Division done.

There were several things missing after his death and I suspect that, true to form, he gave away some of his possessions in preparation. I still have the black ring binder; he had abandoned it to the back of a cupboard, the novel unwritten apart from a few paragraphs full of unspecified despair.

When Ian found his direction, the notebooks, the scraps of paper and the plastic carrier bag became an extension of his body. All he was unable to express on a personal level was poured into his writing, and so his lyrics tell much more than a conversation with him ever could.

Seeing those manuscripts in his distinctive hand and in chronological order goes some way to explain the turmoil he felt. Those human issues and concerns will always be relevant; and although the poetry readily stands alone, his voice and the music that is Joy Division is there to be listened to and absorbed as one perfect body of work as intended.

DEBORAH CURTIS, April 2014

# INTRODUCTION
# BY JON SAVAGE

'Need to ignore + tear up previous influences (unimportant) – look ahead. Taste is habit. The repetition of something already accepted.'

IAN CURTIS, handwritten note about 'Atrocity Exhibition', 1979

A top 20 hit in summer 1980, 'Love Will Tear Us Apart' has since become one of those rare songs that span the classes and generations. It's been covered dozens of times and regularly heads the 'Best of' lists that guide data-overloaded humans through the riches of postwar popular music. It's loved by pop obsessives and those who don't usually pay much attention to music; it's been played on *Coronation Street* and *Match of the Day*. It's become a twentieth-century classic.

Before all that, 'Love Will Tear Us Apart' was a new song. Its first recorded public airing was on 16 October 1979 at Plan K, an arts venue in Brussels. The performance is captured on the VHS footage shot that night by Michel Isbecque: grainy and frazzled, it omits the first minute or so but it shows Ian Curtis slashing out D-chord drones with his back to the audience. He holds his beautiful, white Vox Phantom VI like an unwanted encumbrance, which it was: restricting his body movement, preventing him from letting go.

The new song was heralded by a shift in the group dynamic. Joy Division had occasionally tinkered with their basic guitar/bass/drums line-up – Bernard Sumner and Peter Hook would swap instruments on songs like 'The Sound of Music' – but the introduction of a synthesiser in late summer 1979 demanded another element to fill out the live sound. Ian Curtis had been resistant at first, but took up the guitar to flesh out 'I Remember Nothing', which had become a synthesised epic in concert. The new song cemented Ian's guitar playing as part of the repertoire.

'Love Will Tear Us Apart Again' – as it was first called – was played on and off during the Buzzcocks tour in October. It features in the footage shot by Richard Boon at the Manchester Apollo on 27 October and again in the taped show at the Winter Gardens, Bournemouth on 2 November. The group included a version in their second John Peel session, transmitted on 10 December, and after that it was a fixture in the set – a fan favourite, a sure-fire hit single, the song that was going to break Joy Division and save Factory.

The importance placed upon 'Love Will Tear Us Apart' resulted in a series of recording sessions that were unusually protracted for Joy Division. An early version was taped at Pennine Sound Studios in early January 1980; taken at a concert clip, it was thought un-satisfactory, and the group had another go at Strawberry Studios a couple of months later. The song was finally mixed during the Britannia Row sessions for their second album and was ready to go. By the time it was released in June, it had been overtaken by the events that would retrospectively skew its meaning.

The appeal of 'Love Will Tear Us Apart' lies in its melody, arrange-ment, performance and message. It begins with a bass pulse: the guitar arrives with a dramatic flourish and the drums clatter, before they resolve into a syncopated drum beat and an instantly mem-orable synthesiser figure. It's an old analogue synth, which conveys warmth and alienation at the same time: the melody is at once uplifting and wistful. Curtis's voice has lost its previous punk bark: it's more nuanced, almost crooned – an echo of the Frank Sinatra record supplied by Tony Wilson as a stylistic guide.

The arrangement is deceptively light and airy, but the sentiments are not. The vocal is mixed up high – in comparison to most of 'Unknown Pleasures', where Curtis is *in* there with the group. It's more a solo rather than a rock vocal, and this forces attention, as was intended, on the lyrics. There are three verses. The first states the situation that gives rise to the chorus – 'And we're changing our ways, taking different roads' – while the next two plunge you into the roiling emotions at the end of something that is more than just a love affair: a marriage, or long-term partnership.

The second verse has lines of a startling intimacy: 'Why is the bedroom so cold?/ You've turned away on your side. Is my timing that flawed? Our respect runs so dry.' Curtis kept on returning to themes of blame, shame and guilt throughout the three or so years that he wrote lyrics, but here he applies these themes to a readily identifiable, human predicament: 'You cry out in your sleep/ All my failings exposed/ And there's a taste in my mouth/ As desperation takes hold.'

At the core of the song is the paradox that love and intimacy – 'something so good' – can destroy as well as uplift. And, as the lyric insists, it will continue to do that as long as two people keep on coming back for more, as long as they fail to find a resolution. It's this tension that drives the song: the fact that 'there's still this appeal that we've kept through our lives' makes it hard to break away, but the end result is always the same – 'love *will* tear us apart'. There is a tiny glimmer of hope, but by the end, it has been extinguished.

'Love Will Tear Us Apart' is a remarkable achievement: the intensely personal rendered general. As Curtis's best-known lyric, it has been endlessly dissected in the light of his subsequent suicide in mid May 1980. The single was eventually released in late June, a month and a half later: grief, sadness and press attention helped to push the record into the charts. Once the hardcore fans had bought it, a wider audience took over, pushing the song up to number 13 and keeping it in the charts for two months – the first national hit by Joy Division and for Factory Records.

In the customary narrative, the lyric is thought to refer to the problems in Ian's marriage to Deborah Curtis – prompted by his lifestyle as a musician and his meeting Annik Honoré. The timings would seem to bear that out: 'Love Will Tear Us Apart' was written in the high summer of 1979. Ian first met Annik in August. It was also at this point that Deborah writes of her husband in *Touching From a Distance*: 'As I became familiar with the lyrics [of *Unknown Pleasures*] I worried that Ian was retreating to the depression of his teenage years.'

The almost forensic detail of a disintegrating relationship contained in the lyric seems to reinforce the song's authenticity. But it is a great mistake to think that songwriters always work autobiographically. Rock demands authenticity but the simple fact is most songwriters work in a mode: they assume a voice, or, like fiction writers, imagine a situation that may take elements from their own life but that fights shy of naked autobiography. Pop is distilled emotion, and to reach a wider audience, the personal must be alchemised into something universal.

'Love Will Tear Us Apart' highlights the puzzle that is at the heart of Ian Curtis's lyrics. Are they fiction, or are they autobiography? Are they the product of experience or imagination? Are they artificial or authentic? Did Ian write his own script? Did he predict what was to happen to him? The one thing that is not in question is that, already by his early twenties, Ian Curtis was, in Bernard

Sumner's words, 'a real writer', with his own distinctive voice and his own aesthetic.

Joy Division were a group formed in his vision, which was bookish and dystopian. In the same way that Jim Morrison referenced Louis-Ferdinand Céline's *Journey to the End of the Night* in The Doors' moody masterpiece, 'End of the Night', Curtis dropped hints in song titles like 'Dead Souls', 'Colony', and 'Atrocity Exhibition', which sourced writers as diverse as Nikolai Gogol, Franz Kafka and J. G. Ballard, while the lyrics reflected, in mood and approach, his interests in the horror, science-fiction and experimental genres.

This is not to legitimise Curtis's lyrics as an extension of literature, far from it: they were written to be performed and dramatised on record and in concert. Unlike many writers, he had an audience in front of him acting as a mirror, reacting to what he sang and, as Joy Division was a rock group, all too often assuming that the man and his words were the same thing. This confusion between person and persona would, as the group became more successful and indeed more powerful, cause him great problems.

Ian Curtis was an avid reader who became a driven writer 'Trying to find a clue, trying to find a way to get out'. In the North-West of the mid to late seventies, he found a pop culture that acted as a clearing house for information that was occult in the widest sense: esoteric, degraded, unpopular, underneath the literary radar. There was a whole subculture that supported these endeavours to go underground, to step outside. He found the materials that he needed for his escape, only to discover that – as advised in much of his reading – that escape was impossible.

Like The Doors or The Fall, Joy Division were named from a book. Their inspiration was not Aldous Huxley or Albert Camus, however, but a piece of Holocaust fiction. *House of Dolls* by Ka-Tzetnik (real name Yehiel Feiner) told, in diary form, of the section in a Nazi concentration camp that cast young women into enforced sex slavery: not the Labour Division but the Joy Division. By 1978, when the group adopted their name, this sensationalised memoir had sold millions of copies in paperback.

This kind of pulp history – the Second World War told and retold from every possible perspective – was pumped out in the seventies by publishers like Corgi and Panther: popular items included the series of Wehrmacht and SS novels by Sven Hassel. Bernard Sumner remembers that 'some bloke where I worked at the time gave me five books and that was one of them. One of the others was called *The Knights of Bushido* [by Lord Russell of Liverpool], which was about Japanese atrocities. Another was *Fear of Flying*, by Erica Jong.'

The early to mid seventies was a golden age of paperback publishing. As well as Penguin, with its vigorous science-fiction line that included authors like Philip K. Dick, Olaf Stapledon and J. G. Ballard, there were many others: Picador, Pan, Mayflower, Paladin – the last with a wide-ranging list that included Jeff Nuttall and Timothy Leary. Selling for 50p and upwards (when an LP cost £3.25), these books were readily available to young minds.

In the Manchester area there were several niche outlets for this jumble of esoterica. The historian C. P. Lee remembers shops like Paperchase and the left-wing Grassroots, while Paul Morley worked at The Bookshop in Stockport: 'They would have a science-fiction section, Hal Ellson's *Dangerous Visions*, all the Ballards. Tolkien was a huge seller, war books too, lots of experimental science fiction, as well as the Mills & Boon romances and tucked away soft porn that kept things ticking over. I didn't get educated in school, I got educated in this bookshop.'

Then there were the stores run by David Britton and Mike Butterworth: House on the Borderland, Orbit in Shudehill and finally Bookchain in Peter Street, just down the road from the site of the Peterloo Massacre. As Butterworth recalls: all three 'were modelled on a London bookshop of the period, Dark They Were, and Golden Eyed, in Berwick Street, Soho – which sold comics, sci-fi, drug-related stuff, posters, etc. – and a chain called Popular Books'.

Stephen Morris remembered visiting House on the Borderland while truanting with his friends: 'We just used to go in there and have a right laugh at the old blokes coming in and looking at the porn. There used to be science fiction and weird books and over in a corner there used to be naked ladies. Surprisingly enough the science fiction had little appeal for the vast majority of the clientele, who were going over to the naked-lady corner. I'd just be trying to negotiate some kind of discount on a large expensive book.'

Butterworth remembers Stephen Morris and Ian Curtis – who both visited House on the Borderland on separate occasions – as 'disparate, alienated young men attracted to like-minded souls. They wanted something offbeat and off the beaten track, and the shop supplied this, not only the staff who manned the counter but also some of the customers who came in. They probably saw the shop as being a beacon in the rather bleak Manchester of the early seventies.'

'The attitude radiating from the shop was *fuck everybody in authority*', Butterworth stated in a 2008 interview, 'and that's what they responded to.' As he told me, 'they came in every couple of weeks, sometimes more often. Ian bought second-hand copies of *New Worlds*, the great sixties literary magazine edited by Michael Moorcock, which was promoting Burroughs and Ballard. My friendship with Ian started around 1979: we talked Burroughs, Burroughs, Burroughs. At the bookshops he would have been exposed to an extremely wide range of eclectic and weird writers and music.'

Born and raised in Macclesfield, Ian Curtis won a scholarship to the prestigious King's School but dropped out of full-time education at the age of seventeen. As an autodidact, he took his cues from the pop culture of the time. In 1974, David Bowie was interviewed with William Burroughs in *Rolling Stone*. The actual chat was fairly non-eventful, but it made the link between literature and music explicit – especially when Bowie was seen fiddling with cut-ups in Alan Yentob's *Cracked Actor* documentary – and Burroughs would cast a major shadow over British Punk and Post Punk.

In the mid seventies, there was a sense – reinforced by the vacant, derelict inner cities – that the bomb had already dropped. With its casual brutality and black humour, Burroughs's accelerated prose – what biographer Ted Morgan called his 'nuclear style' – matched this apocalyptic mood. The lack of conventional narrative in his books plunged the reader into a maelstrom of malevolent, unseen forces and ever-present, unidentified dangers. At the same time, there was a sense that, like in *The Wild Boys*, this was an environment in which the young could run wild.

Joy Division rarely did interviews. In January 1980, however, they gave an audience to the young writer and singer Alan Hempsall. This was the only time that Ian would talk on record about his reading, and he cited *The Naked Lunch* and *The Wild Boys* among his favourites. The group had recently encountered Burroughs at their Plan K show in October 1979: however when Curtis approached the great man to get a free copy of *The Third Mind*, a collaboration with Brion Gysin that had been published the previous year, he was summarily dismissed.

Ian Curtis had grown up with a love of books. One of his childhood favourites was *A Century of Thrillers: from Poe to Arlen*, a *Daily Express* compendium published in 1934. Stephen Morris remembered Ian having *The Atrocity Exhibition*, *The Naked Lunch*, and 'a collection of Jim Morrison's poems. He would proudly show you where Iggy had stolen 'The Passenger' from: "Look, he's nicked it off Jim Morrison." I seem to remember that you could go to [W. H.] Smith's and they had Burroughs and Ballard mixed in with the rest of the stuff.'

Curtis began writing in earnest during 1977, when he and Deborah got their first proper home together, in Barton Street, Macclesfield. At the time, he was working for the Manpower Services Commission, so any writing had to be done at night. Deborah remembers that 'we prepared the triangular room of our new home for the composition of Ian's forthcoming masterpieces. He painted the walls sky blue, the carpet was blue, the three-seater settee was blue, as were the curtains. The only concession was the bright red spotlights and, later, a red telephone.'

'Most nights Ian would go into the blue room and shut the door behind him to write, interrupted only by my cups of coffee handed in through the swirls of Marlboro smoke. I didn't mind the situation; we regarded it as a project, something that had to be done. Neither did I inspect his work. I never doubted that his songs would be anything but superior.'

Ian Curtis wrote his lyrics by hand, first in small notebooks, and later on loose leaf sheets of A4 paper. All but seven of the Joy Division songs that he wrote exist in some handwritten form: with very few exceptions, he wrote in capitals. His hand was distinctive. In the various drafts, notes, set lists, album titles and alternative versions, it's possible to see the germ of various completed songs – for instance an early attempt called 'This Is My Crisis' becomes 'Passover' – as well as explanations of his dystopian worldview.

His first attempts showed a writer struggling to establish a style. One of Joy Division's most effective early recordings, 'No Love Lost', contains a spoken word section that lifts a complete paragraph from *The House of Dolls*: this fits the relentless yet spacious Motorik of the music extremely well. Other 1977 songs like 'Leaders of Men', 'Warsaw', 'Conditioned' and 'Crime Against the Innocents' were barely digested regurgitations of their sources: lumpy screeds of frustration, guilt, shame and anger with militarist and totalitarian overtones.

An early song like 'The Drawback' shows, in a raw form, the themes that Ian Curtis would mine deep: 'I've seen the products and the other world of waste/ I've seen the colour of corruption deep within/ I've seen them lose themselves in dignity and taste/

To see in black and white and through to black again.' Like many intelligent young people, Curtis emerged into a world that he had not made, the wrongs of which he could see clearly: 'I'm so cold and tired with our society,' he wrote in a lyric called 'Clutch At Straws'. 'I'll wake this dormant sleep + this complacency.'

Like his colleagues, Curtis worked hard to improve, to move beyond bad punk into something more striking and individual, more fitting his lyrical themes. His keynote song for early Joy Division was 'Shadowplay', which they played on Granada television in June 1978. Like a Burroughs cut-up, the lyrics shifted from a direct address to a description of a situation – often horrific or unsettling: 'the assassins all grouped in four lines' – sealed with a first-person confession of guilt or helplessness – 'I did everything, everything I wanted to/ I let them use you for their own ends.'

But the most iconic line was the first: 'To the centre of the city where all roads meet, waiting for you'. Both in words and music, Joy Division mapped the depressed city of Manchester, an environment at once degraded and deserted but, in a strange way, futuristic. Granada emphasised the spatial aspect of the song by inserting negative footage of cars driving around Washington, taken from a *World In Action* documentary about the CIA. Control and ambience all came together in the group's first television appearance.

By then, Curtis was exploring more than horror and Nazi exploitation. Among his books were volumes by T. S. Eliot and Antonin Artaud. Deborah remembers him reading 'Dostoyevsky, Nietzsche, Jean-Paul Sartre, Hermann Hesse and J. G. Ballard. *Photomontages of the Nazi Period* was a book of anti-Nazi posters by John Heartfield, which graphically documented the spread of Hitler's ideals. *Crash* by J. G. Ballard combined sex with the suffering of car accident victims.' Another favourite was Ballard's 1975 *High Rise*.

Deborah recently recalled that Ian never read these books in her presence. She felt this was 'an indication to me that he considered them part of his work. They were important to him. It wasn't something he did as relaxation or for pleasure. He was studying/working. Too important to try and concentrate on with someone else in the room. It wasn't something he did as relaxation or for pleasure. His books would be on the floor next to his drafts . . . He continually searched for influences, situations he could put himself in.'

At Joy Division rehearsals, Ian Curtis would act as the director, spotting riffs and working with the others to turn them into structured songs. As Stephen Morris remembers: 'We'd do these long rambling jam things and Ian would just sit in a corner with his book of words and try out some of the words he'd written. He'd come out with words and immediately it sounded less like a rambling jam and more like a song. In the course of an afternoon we could come up with a song or two, because he had so many lyrics.'

From the start, Curtis was determined to go deeper than the average pop or punk lyric. 'Ian was into the extremities of life,' Bernard Sumner told me in 1994; 'He wanted to make extreme music, and he wanted to be totally extreme onstage, no half measures. My influence was from my grandparents and the war. Ian's influence seemed to be madness and insanity. He said that his sister, or his aunt, had worked in a mental home, and she used to tell him things about the people in the mental home: people with twenty nipples or two heads, and that left a big impression on him'.

From mid 1978 onwards, the words poured out of him. Curtis did not seek conventional narratives but sought instead to create a situation in which the emotion came from the response of the narrator. Within these fictional scenarios, the 'I' was often trapped, as in a Greek tragedy, by forces outside his control: 'I've seen the nights, filled with bloodsport and pain' ('Day of the Lords'); 'I don't care any more/ I've lost the will to want more' ('Insight'); 'Different colours, different shades/ Over each mistakes were made/ I took the blame' ('New Dawn Fades').

Like many young men, Curtis oscillated between feelings of omnipotence and abjection, and his lyrics and his writings reflected this. On the one hand he wanted to shake things up, but on the other he felt helpless, 'threatened by life itself'. In the loose leaf sheets there are try-out lyric notes like 'I witnessed the death of 1000 young men, but couldn't do nothing at all', or 'mass murder on a grand scale mass graves a man who couldn't cope'.

The sense of a hero struggling within a labyrinthine system is a common theme in Kafka, Gogol and Burroughs, amongst others. It's not hard to see a thematic line from Kafka's Control Officials ('The Castle') to Burroughs's theories of Control, or from the fatalism of the nineteenth-century Russians to postwar science fiction. In this, Ballard's exquisite techno-barbarism offered another twist. Science fiction offers an alternative present, and Curtis used this language on Joy Division's first album, *Unknown Pleasures*.

In Ian's notes there is a list of alternative titles: the album could have been called *From the Wilderness*, *Symptoms of Collapse*, *Will of the Underworld*, *Cause for Anxiety*, *Convulsive Therapy* or *Passover*. In the ten songs he travels through time and space, through a visionary landscape that begins in the knowable – late seventies'

Manchester – but ends up in the dark recesses of the imagination, in trials of law and of strength, in guilt, despair and isolation. 'Guess your dreams always end', he sang on 'Insight', 'They don't rise up just descend.'

At this point Ian Curtis was still fictionalising his reading and his experience. 'Interzone' took a word from Burroughs and used it to place desperate and forgotten youth in empty, grid-like Mancunian landscapes. The intimate connection between the group and their environment was sealed by Charles Salem's 8mm film, *No City Fun*, which set grainy, washed-out images of bleak Hulme and spiritually impoverished central Manchester – still struggling to escape from the recession – to the first side of *Unknown Pleasures*. It was a perfect fit.

'She's Lost Control' was taken from an incident at Curtis's workplace. As Sumner recalls: 'Part of the time when Joy Division was forming, he worked in a rehabilitation centre for people with physical and mental disabilities, trying to find work again. He was very much affected by those people. "She's Lost Control" was about a girl who used to come in to the centre and try to find work. She had epilepsy and lost more and more time through it, and then one day she just didn't come in any more. He assumed that she'd found a job, but found out later that she'd had a fit and died.'

At the same time, *Unknown Pleasures* showed a preoccupation with religious imagery and martyrdom, mixed with a Nietzschean aloofness. Curtis was at once a revolutionary idealist, energised by Punk (part of him hoped to make a difference, to 'burn the old ideals'), and a deep, deep pessimist who saw no hope: maybe he was on 'an expedition doomed to fail'. It's not hard to see how Curtis would have identified with the civil-servant hero of Dostoyevsky's *Notes From Underground*, with his nihilistic disdain for the human 'anthill': 'We are born dead.'

There's an uncomfortable side to Curtis's early lyrics – a preoccupation with totalitarian imagery and thought. There were songs like 'Warsaw' and 'They Walked In Line'; in his notes are phrases like 'steel + willpower guns + firepower', 'Level of Violence', 'Aura of Retribution', 'Cleansing of the Soul', 'Twilight of the Idols'. It's possible to be fascinated with the topic without taking on the ideology – and indeed there was an element of trying to understand what had happened in then recent history – but this obsession added to the dark clouds that were beginning to cluster.

Ian Curtis was, of course, ill: he was an epileptic, and his condition was worsening as the group became more successful from mid

1979 onwards. His lyrics were only part of the package. Joy Division were a total artwork, right down to the record sleeves, the clothes and their posters. Live, they were brutal and impossibly intense: as a front man, Curtis placed himself completely in the moment with a persona that, intentionally or not, approximated the faraway stare of a seer: 'I travelled far and wide through many different times.' ('Wilderness')

In the pivotal 'Atrocity Exhibition', he wrote 'For entertainment they watch his body twist/ Behind his eyes he says, "I still exist"'. Although it refers to Ballard's novella, the mood of the song takes from Hermann Hesse's *Steppenwolf* and could be applied to Curtis's own experience as a mediumistic performer. When asked about this by Alan Hempsall in January 1980, Curtis replied that he'd written the song way before he'd read the book: 'I just saw this title and thought that it fitted with the ideas of the lyrics.'

It seems clear that Curtis used his books as mood generators, as portals into the other worlds and other times that he sought to inhabit. Deborah had begun by being supportive but began to worry that 'all Ian's spare time was spent reading and thinking about human suffering. I knew he was looking for inspiration for his songs, yet the whole thing was culminating in an unhealthy obsession with mental and physical pain.' As she recently wrote: 'I think that reading those books must have really nurtured his "sad" side.'

Premiered that summer at the Factory Club, 'Dead Souls' (a title taken from the book by Nikolai Gogol) was a slice of H. P. Lovecraft horror, old and cold, that made the hairs stand up on your neck. It told of visions that came unbidden, that could not be turned off: 'Someone take these dreams away/ That point me to another day'. With its long, two-minute introduction, Joy Division would often use it to open their set: it allowed Ian to limber up onstage, to gauge the mood of the audience, and then to project himself forward and outward however he wished. It was a gateway song.

In July and August, Joy Division were in increasing demand. As the pressure built up, Deborah remembers in *Touching From a Distance* that 'Ian's fits became more frequent and I found it increasingly difficult to communicate with him . . . I found myself shut out of Ian's problems. His resentment towards me seemed to be building. Perhaps it was my imagination, but I thought he held me responsible for his condition. I knew nothing of the mental side effects of his therapy and even if I did, would not have expected such an adverse effect on Ian's personality.'

It was at this point that Ian Curtis wrote 'Love Will Tear Us Apart', the song which would mark the change in Joy Division's brief, intense life. It was not only an obvious signature tune, but it also seemed to mark the point where Ian Curtis's lyrics became more personally oriented and less fictive. He had begun by assuming a standpoint taken from his reading but from autumn 1979 on would become increasingly directed inward, into his own turmoil. His lyrics became less about situations and more about psychological states.

Deborah felt that 'the lyrics Ian chose to match the band's already haunting music were increasingly depressive; if you wanted to believe that he was writing about someone's experience, then you also had to believe that he was capable of enormous empathy. Journalists and fans alike tried to decipher his words and now, of course, many feel that Ian's melancholy was staring them in the face. It was too incredible to comprehend that he would use such a public method to cry for help.'

She well observes the slippage into autobiography marked by 'Love Will Tear Us Apart': '*Your bedroom, this bedroom, the bedroom*: he played with these variations. Was he trying to depersonalise the lyrics or did he genuinely not know which bedroom he was referring to? Of course, now I can see that it was another situation he could draw on and not that different to writing about a tragedy he might see on the news; but the burden of finding a way to displace what was happening in his life must have twisted him to the core.'

As Ian Curtis's epilepsy worsened under the stress of being a successful musician, his lyrics began to mirror his despair. 'Nothing seems real anymore,' he wrote at the time in one of the notes kept with his lyrics. 'Even the flames from the fire seem to beckon to me, drawing me in to some great past life buried somewhere deep in my subconscious, if only I could find the key . . . if only . . . if only. Ever since my illness, my condition, I've been trying to find some logical way of passing my time, of justifying a means to an end.'

There were signs. Bernard Sumner recalls an incident from the Buzzcocks tour: 'We played in Bournemouth, and his mate, who was this performance artist, didn't turn up at the gig and Ian was really upset. The Buzzcocks were staying in this shitty hotel, and we walked along to their hotel for a drink, and coming back along the beach Ian starting walking out towards the sea. It was pitch black, about one in the morning, and he went walking into the sea, and we had to go and get him. He had a shadow on his personality, that was so dark that I don't think even he could see into it.'

But none of the group or those around them reacted to this change: they were used to Ian's darkness of tone or didn't think about the lyrics at all – that was his contribution to the group effort. Busy with their own tasks, they didn't discuss the matter, nor were the lyrics printed or broadcast in any way. 'We do not particularly like publishing our lyrics,' manager Rob Gretton wrote in autumn 1979; 'because we would like the listener to put some effort into trying to understand them.' It was all part of the mystique: withhold, give nothing away.

'When we heard them, we knew they were very, very good,' Peter Hook remembers. 'His lyrics were very open, weren't they? He was telling a lot about himself, his fears and his doubts, but you were too young and caught up with the excitement of the success of it, it was like a snowball going downhill. It's a great shame because you should have been able to just hear it and say Ian, can we have a chat with you . . . you know? What's the matter? But it comes down to youth, when you're young, you don't tend to notice a lot of things.'

Partly it was the time, partly it was the place and the culture: people didn't talk about psychological states in late seventies Manchester. The medicine for epilepsy was still primitive. But most of all, it was Ian Curtis himself, who refused to reveal the seriousness of his condition and the pressures that he was under – juggling his illness, his marriage, and his responsibilities to the group. 'Ian would always say what he thought you wanted to hear,' Stephen Morris remembers. 'He was really nice. He'd never say anything nasty to anybody. He wouldn't like upsetting people.'

As was his prerogative, Ian resisted interpretation. He was, as Morris remembers, 'pretty private about what he wrote'. He hardly ever talked about his lyrics, and when he did, avoided too much detail: in an interview in the fanzine *Printed Noises*, he stated that 'we haven't got a message really, the lyrics are open to interpretation. They're multi-dimensional. You can read into them what you like. Obviously they're important to the band.' Deborah remembers that 'Ian had always enjoyed reading into other people's lyrics'.

Even so, she felt concerned enough to raise the subject with her husband, zeroing on the line 'but I remember when we were young': 'Ian sounded old, as if he had lived a lifetime in his youth. After pondering over the words to "New Dawn Fades", I broached the subject with Ian, trying to make him confirm that they were only lyrics and bore no resemblance to his real feelings. It was a one-sided conversation. He refused to confirm or deny any of the points raised and he walked out of the house.'

By the beginning of 1980, Joy Division had been professional musicians for three months. Since the recording of *Unknown Pleasures*, they had been writing and recording more and more new songs: 'Dead Souls', 'Atmosphere', and, a rare joyous release, 'Transmission'. Curtis began to perform lyrics which, when heard in concert and combined with his totally committed performances, seemed to apply to his own situation: 'this life isn't mine' ('Something Must Break'); 'Systematically degraded/ Emotionally a scapegoat/ I can't see it getting better' ('The Sound of Music').

In the new year, the group prepared a second full album. A couple of the songs had been concert staples: 'Colony' and 'Atrocity Exhibition' – a key live track with its rippling can-like rhythm. But other, newer lyrics showed the lyrical balance tipping into outright, anguished confessional: 'This is a crisis I knew had to come' ('Passover'); 'Gotta find my destiny, before it gets too late' ('Twenty Four Hours'); 'Existence, well what does it matter? I exist on the best terms I can/ The past is now part of my future/ The present is well out of hand' ('Heart and Soul').

'The Eternal' was inspired by Ian's experience, as Bernard Sumner recalls: 'I remember him telling me that when he was at school in Macclesfield, he used to walk past a house with a garden at the front every day, and there was a young kid with Down's syndrome in that garden. He moved away from Macclesfield for a number of years and came back when he was an adult. He walked past the garden and the little boy was still there, playing. He said it was very strange because he hadn't appeared to have aged at all, but Ian had obviously grown much older. That struck him.'

Although there is always room for ambiguity, it's hard to avoid the conclusion that some of these lyrics were highly personal: instead of placing himself in an imaginary, extreme situation, Ian Curtis is right within the turmoil. On 'Komakino', a song inspired by Joy Division's trip to Berlin that didn't make the album, he sang: 'How can I find the right way to control/ All the conflict inside, all the problems beside/ As the questions arise, and the answers don't fit'.

Ian Curtis's teenage idols included Lou Reed, Iggy Pop and Jim Morrison – all extreme and charismatic performers who aroused powerful feelings and who appeared to hold nothing back. Just as, in concert, he gave all his energy – often ending up exhausted or ill after or even during the show – he had lost any sense of distance, or perspective between his performance and his life. However, rather than acting as a release or an exorcism of his problems, the new material only seemed to embed him further into a spiral of hopelessness.

Bernard Sumner: 'I remember talking to him one very late night in the *Closer* sessions, we were working with Martin at Britannia Row in Islington, and Ian was saying to me that doing this album felt very strange because he felt that all his words were writing themselves. He'd always in the past struggled to finish a song, like he'd have the start but he'd always struggled to complete it, but he just had the whole song straight off. At the same time he had this terrible claustrophobic feeling that he was in a whirlpool and that he was being pulled down.'

These lyrics – both draft and complete – were written to be sung with loud music that was at once brutal and unwavering, futuristic and increasingly sophisticated. They show a distinctive writing talent, cut short, that could well have flourished into middle age and beyond. Bernard Sumner thinks that if Ian 'hadn't committed suicide, he would probably have written a really good book'. Instead, there is a legacy of over forty songs that continue to resonate in the twenty-first century, together with notes and other prose fragments that give extra clues on how those songs were written.

Above all, the lyrics are the work of a young man of twenty-one, twenty-two and twenty-three. They capture the heightened emotions of a particular post-teenage state: the desire to be different and the searching for oddity and extremity, the violent mood swings between feeling omnipotent and hopeless, the dreadful sense that you're never quite good enough, that you're letting everyone down, and the immersion in books as an inspiration and a method, if you feel weird or different, of staving off isolation – 'other people have felt like this, I'm not alone'.

Curtis felt himself emerging into a hostile world outside his control: 'We're living by your rules/ That's all we know'. A powerful strand that weaves through the songs is the idea of 'forgotten youth' in a degraded, hostile society: in the late seventies, young people were at the sharp end of the neo-liberal economic and social experiment. As he wrote: 'corruption – music biz, government business – everything. Dual standards hypocrisy restrictions those with no choice – social or intellectual position holds no bright prospects for future. Trapped in corners – solitary'.

Ian Curtis's great lyrical achievement was to capture the underlying reality of a society in turmoil, and to make it both universal and personal. He felt the human cost of the economic and social restructuring that was occurring in the late seventies – and that still casts its malign shadow today. Distilled emotion is the essence of pop music and, just as Joy Division are perfectly poised between white light and dark despair, so Curtis's lyrics oscillate between hopelessness and the possibility of, if not absolute need for, human connection.

JON SAVAGE, April 2014

'Reality is only a term, based on values and well worn principles, whereas the dream goes on forever.'

IAN CURTIS, handwritten note, circa 1979

# EDITORIAL NOTE:
# DEBORAH CURTIS AND JON SAVAGE

The previous printings of the lyrics – in Deborah Curtis's *Touching From a Distance* and the *Heart and Soul* box set – show that there are forty-five Joy Division songs in total. *Touching From a Distance* prints an early version of the 'The Kill' while the box set prints 'The Drawback' (from the RCA 1978 sessions). The order we have chosen substantially duplicates the chronological sequence in both sources.

Handwritten versions of all the Joy Division lyrics are included in the book except for 'Novelty' – the lyrics of which were written by Peter Hook – and the following missing seven: 'The Drawback', 'Digital', 'Insight', 'Wilderness', 'Decades', 'Ceremony' and 'In a Lonely Place'.

The handwritten lyrics come from several sources: an A4-size ring binder with a few sheets, three small notebooks and a large sheaf of A4-size paper containing about about one-hundred sheets. Two thirds of these have writing on both sides, and you will see traces of this in some of the scans.

It's not possible to do an exact dating, but the pages in the ring binder seem to be the very first lyric writings. The three notebooks seem to cover the early period of Joy Division – 1977–78 – while the loose leaf sheets cover the period from early 1979 until spring 1980.

Finished songs in the chronologically ordered notebooks include:

NOTEBOOK 1 Leaders of Men, Ice Age Version 1, Warsaw, Ice Age Version 2, Failures, Exercise One (Looking at Life), Shadowplay, Interzone, The Kill, They Walked in Line
NOTEBOOK 2 Disorder, Glass, She's Lost Control, Transmission, New Dawn Fades
NOTEBOOK 3 Passover

– the rest are contained in undated loose sheets.

Even so, the lyrics are somewhat of a jigsaw puzzle. Some songs – like 'Passover' or 'Colony' – were worked on over a long time, through different versions. Lyric ideas may appear in the early draft of one song, only to appear late in another. There are a few swapped titles: an early version of 'Shadowplay' is entitled 'Interzone'.

It's clear that Ian worked hard on his lyrics, and had a bank of phrases and ideas that he frequently returned to. One-off lines or rejects would be used later. Very little was left to waste.

In selecting the handwritten drafts of each lyric, we have used the most complete version possible. In a few cases, this means a very rough sketch – most obviously in the note for 'No Love Lost' – but in general, fairly complete drafts exist for most of the songs. Alternatives and try-outs will be found in Appendix One.

In selecting the pages for Appendix One, we have focused on unreleased songs as well as early/alternative drafts of Joy Division recordings. These are arranged in chronological order – based on the source and the date of each song's release – with the songs first, and then some additional prose writings at the back. These include set lists, lists of early songs, and some prose writings. About 90 per cent of the notebook pages and the loose sheets have been used, with edits where there is too much reduplication and, in a very few cases, personal material (phone numbers etc.)

The contents of Appendix Two come from all that is left of Ian's archive: some label proofs, handbills for Joy Division concerts, pages from the fanzines *Acrylic Daze*, *City Fun*, and *London's Outrage*, a selection of books from Ian's library, much of which has been scattered to the winds, and a few letters including two fan-created record covers. It is hoped that this gives some insight into the context and the inspiration for Ian Curtis's lyrics.

JON SAVAGE AND DEBORAH CURTIS, April 2014

# THE HANDWRITTEN LYRICS

## 31G - 350125

I WAS THERE ON THE BACKSTAGE
WHEN THE FIRST LIGHT CAME
AROUND,
  I GREW UP, NOT A
CHANGELING, ~~JUST~~ TO WIN THE
~~FIRST~~ ~~SECOND~~ TIME ROUND
  I CAN SEE ALL THE WEAKNESS
  I CAN PICK ALL THE FAULTS
  BUT I CONCEDE ALL THE FAITH
TESTS,
                    STICK IN
  JUST TO ~~SHOUT~~ AT YOUR THROAT

  I HUNG AROUND IN
YOUR SOUNDTRACK,
  TO MIRROR ALL THAT
YOU'VE DONE
  TO FIND THE RIGHT SIDE
OF REASON,

TO KILL THE THREE LIES
FOR ONE,
I CAN SEE ALL THE
COLD FACTS,
I CAN SEE THROUGH
YOUR EYES
ALL ~~THIS WAY~~ TALK MADE NO
CONTACT,
NO MATTER HOW HARD
~~YOU~~ I TRIED.

I CAN STILL HEAR
THE FOOTSTEPS,
~~████████████~~
I CAN SEE ONLY WALLS
I SLID INTO YOUR
MANTRAPS,
WITH NO MEANING AT ALL.
I JUST SEE CONTRADICTION
I HAD TO   GIVE UP

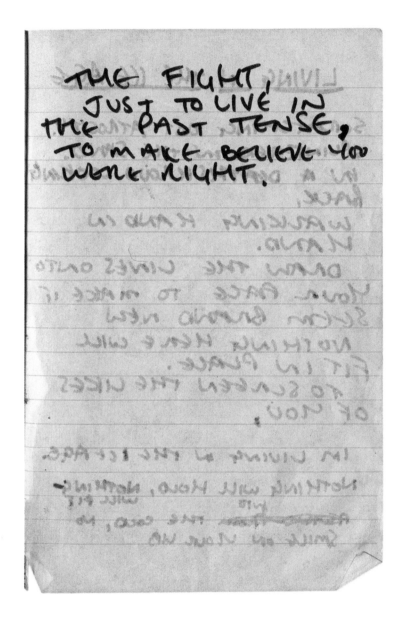

THE FIGHT,
JUST TO LIVE IN
THE PAST TENSE,
TO MAKE BELIEVE YOU
WERE RIGHT.

## WARSAW (1977)

3, 5, 0, 1, 2, 5, Go!

I was there in the back stage
When first light came around.
I grew up like a changeling
To win the first time around
I can see all the weakness
I can pick all the faults
Well I concede all the faith tests
Just to stick in your throats

31G, 31G, 31G

I hung around in your soundtrack
To mirror all that you've done
To find the right side of reason
To kill the three lies for one
I can see all the cold facts
I can see through your eyes
All this talk made no contact
No matter how hard we tried

31G, 31G, 31G

I can still hear the footsteps
I can see only walls
I slid into your man-traps
With no hearing at all
I just see contradiction
Had to give up the fight
Just to live in the past tense
To make believe you were right

31G, 31G, 31G

3, 5, 0, 1, 2, 5.

<u>Leaders of Men</u>

Born from some mothers womb
just like any other room
made a promise for a new life
made a victim out of your life

When your times on the door
and it drips to the floor
and you feel that you can touch
but the noise is too much
and the seeds that are sown
are no longer your own

Just a minor operation
to force the final ultimatum

thousand words are spoken loud
reach the dumb to fool the crowds

When you walk down the street
then the sounds not so sweet
and you wish you could hide
maybe go for a ride
to some peep show arcade
where the futures not made

A nightmare situation
To infiltrate imagination
smacks of pasts holy wars
by the wall with broken laws

Leaders of man, made a promise of a new life
    "    "    "    made a wreckage out of your life
    "    "    ""    born out of your frustation
    "    "    "    just a strange infatuation

No saviour for our sakes

to crush the internees of hate

self induced manipulation

to crush all thoughts of mass salvation.

I. Curtis

(July, 1977, Copyright).

# LEADERS OF MEN (1977)

Born from some mother's womb
Just like any other room
Made a promise for a new life
Made a victim out of your life

When your time's on the door
And it drips to the floor
And you feel you can touch
All the noise is too much
And the seeds that are sown
Are no longer your own

Just a minor operation
To force a final ultimatum
Thousand words are spoken loud
Reach the dumb to fool the crowd

When you walk down the street
And the sound's not so sweet
And you wish you could hide
Maybe go for a ride
To some peep show arcade
Where the future's not made

A nightmare situation
Infiltrate imagination
Smacks of past holy wars
By the wall with broken laws

The leaders of men
Born out of your frustration
The leaders of men
Just a strange infatuation
The leaders of men
Made a promise for a new life
No saviour for our sakes
To twist the internees of hate
Self-induced manipulation
To crush all thoughts of mass salvation.

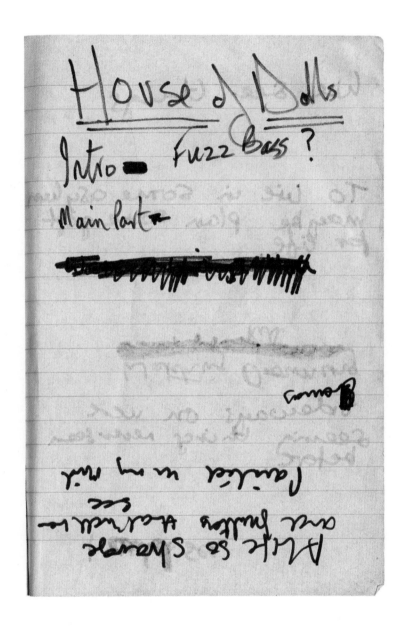

# House of Dolls

Intro — Fuzz Bass ?

Main Part —

Underground
~~Soundtrack~~

So long settlin here
didn't ~~hear~~ the warnings
waitin for the tape to
                    run.

                    moving
We've been ~~hanging~~
round,
I'm a different situa
~~knowing~~
~~keeping~~ that the time
would come.

Just to see you torn
apart
    Witness to your empty.
heart.
    for now.

## NO LOVE LOST (1977)

So long sitting here
Didn't hear the warning
Waiting for the tape to run
We've been moving around in different situations
Knowing that the time would come
Just to see you torn apart
Witness to your empty heart
I need it
I need it
I need it
Through the wire screen, the eyes of those standing outside
   looked in at her as into the cage of some rare creature in a zoo
In the hand of one of the assistants she saw the same instrument
   which they had that morning inserted deep into her body. She
   shuddered instinctively. No life at all in the house of dolls
No love lost. No love lost.

You've been seeing things
In darkness, not in learning
Hoping that the truth will pass
No life underground, wasting never changing
Wishing that this day won't last.
To never see you show your age
To watch until the beauty fades
I need it.
I need it.
I need it.

(Second verse on *Warsaw* album)
Two-way mirror in the hall
They like to watch everything you do
Transmitters hidden in the walls
So they know everything you say is true
Turn it on
Don't turn it on
Turn it on.

## FAILURES OF THE MODERN MAN

Don't speak of safe Messiah,
A Failure of the modern
man,
To the centre of all
lifes desires,
As a whole not an
also ran.

Love in a hollow field
Break the image of
your fathers son,
Drawn to an inner feel,
He was thought of as
the only one.

He no longer denies
All the failures of the
Modern Man.

No now we can't pick
sides
    Sees the failures of
the Modern Man.

Wise words and sympathy
tell the story of our
history,
New strength gives a
real touch,
With ~~good~~ sense it reason makes
it all too much,

Now that the time to decide,
In his time he was the
only one,
Taken from Caesars side,
Kept in silence just to
prove whos wrong.

    He no longer denies
        eu:

# FAILURES (1977)

Don't speak of safe Messiahs
A failure of the Modern Man
To the centre of all life's desires
As a whole not an also ran
Love in a hollow field
Break the image of your father's son
Drawn to an inner feel
He was thought of as the only one
He was thought of as the only one

He no longer denies
All the failures of the Modern Man
No, no, no, he can't pick sides
Sees the failures of the Modern Man
Wise words and sympathy
Tell the story of our history
New strength gives a real touch
Sense and reason make it all too much
With a strange fatality
Broke the spirits of a lesser man
Some other race can see
In his way he was the only one
In his way he was the only one

He no longer denies
All the failures of the Modern Man
No, no, no, he can't pick sides
Sees the failures of the Modern Man
Now that it's right to decide
In his time he was a total man
Taken from Caesar's side
Kept in silence just to prove who's wrong
He no longer denies
All the failures of the Modern Man
No, no, no, he can't pick sides
Sees the failures of the Modern Man
All the failures of the Modern Man.

# ICE AGE

WE SAW THE REAL
ATROCITIES,
  BURIED IN THE SAND,
STOCKPILED SAFETY FOR
JUST A FEW,
  WHILE WE STOOD HOLDING
HANDS.

  WERE SEARCHIN FOR
SOME OTHER WAY,
  WE'LL HIDE BEHIND THE
DOOR.
  ~~THEN~~ WE'LL LIVE
IN ~~CAVES~~ HOLES AND DISEASED SHACKS
WITH HOPES FOR LITTLE
MORE

# ICE AGE (1977)

I've seen the real atrocities
Buried in the sand
Stockpiled safety for a few
While we stand holding hands

I'm living in the Ice age
I'm living in the Ice age
Nothing will hold
Nothing will fit
Into the cold
It's not an eclipse
Living in the Ice age
Living in the Ice age
Living in the Ice age

Searching for another way
Hide behind the door
We'll live in holes and disused shafts
Hopes for little more

I'm living in the Ice age
I'm living in the Ice age
Nothing will hold
Nothing will fit
Into the cold
No smile on your lips
Living in the Ice age
Living in the Ice age
Living in the Ice age
Living in the Ice age
Living in the Ice age
Living in the Ice age
Living in the Ice age.

The Kill

Keep it all clean,
that's what he said.
No kings of ~~gut~~ ~~misuse~~,
sellers of flesh,
I had my own dream.
where trees lined the
street, the only things
bought was the food that
you eat

I had an impulse
to clear it away,
I'll use their tactics, to make
them all pay,
I'm disposable ~~spend~~
my tires at the wheel,
No point in living
can't do what you feel.

# THE KILL (1977)

Moved in a hired car
And I find no way to run
Adds every moment longer
Had no time for fun
Just something that I knew I had to do
But through it all I left my eyes on you.

I had an impulse to clear it all away
Oh I used the tactics, make everybody pay
Just something that I knew I had to do
But through it all I kept my eyes on you.

Oh, I keep it all clean
I've paid the graces there
No kings of misuse
No sellers of flesh
Just something that I knew I had to do
But through it all I kept my eyes on you
Yeah through it all I kept my eyes on you
But through it all I kept my eyes on you.

*Dawn Patrol Parade*

All dressed in uniforms so
fine, drank
    *They were the*
They ~~—~~ + killed to pass
the time,
Wearing the shame of all their
crimes,
   With measured steps they
walked in line.

*They walked in lines*
*they walked in lines*
*They walked in lines*
*They walked in lines*

*They walked in lines*
*they walked in lines*

They carried pictures of their
wives,
  And numbered tags to
prove their lives,

And made it through the
whale machine
With dirty ~~hands~~ but
~~hands~~, so clean.

~~Out into shadows ur~~
~~to right~~
~~they did what they had~~
~~thought was right.~~

For love of glory
never seen.
And, ~~and~~
They made it through the
~~uniformed boys~~ they
plunged in deep whale machine
To never question
any more,
W~~~~
To never ~~~~ cope of what
they saw.

# THEY WALKED IN LINE (1978)

All dressed in uniforms so fine
They drank and killed to pass the time
Wearing the shame of all their crimes
With measured steps, they walked in line

They walked in line
They walked in line
They walked in line
They walked in line . . .

They carried pictures of their wives
And numbered tags to prove their lives

They walked in line
They walked in line
They walked in line
They walked in line . . .

Full of a glory never seen
They made it through the whole machine
To never question any more
Hypnotic trance, they never saw

They walked in line
They walked in line
They walked in line
They walked in line . . .
They walked in a line
They walked in line
They walked in line
They walked in line
They walked in line
They walked in line
Walked in line
Walked in line.

## LOOKIN AT LIFE.

When your lookin at life
Thru an empty room,
Some strange new room.
Is this the start of it all
    thats

Too Turn down the TV.
Turn down your pulse,
Set Controls on your heart
Cos its getting too much.
  maybe

Yeah your lookin at life
Deciphering scars,
Just who fools who,
Sat still in their cars.

And the lights look bright,
When you reach outside,
All these years at yar sid
Thats the start of it all
              end

# EXERCISE ONE (1978)

When you're looking at life
In a strange new room
Maybe drowning soon
Is this the start of it all?
Turn on your TV
Turn down your pulse
Turn away from it all
It's all getting too much.

When you're looking at life
Deciphering scars
Just who fooled who
Sit still in their cars
The lights look bright
When you reach outside
Time for one last ride
Before the end of it all.

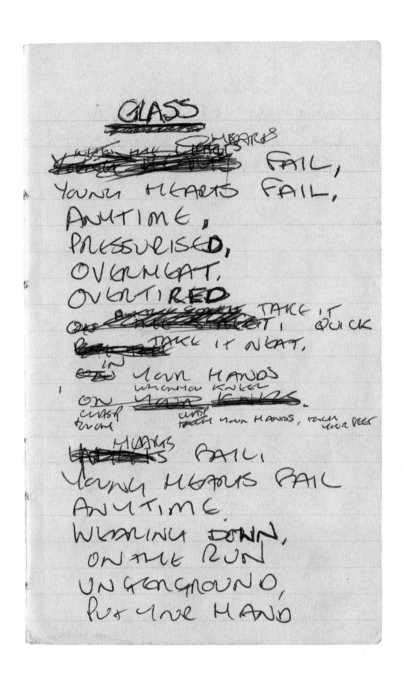

# GLASS

~~YOUNG HEARTS~~
~~YOUNG HEARTS~~ FAIL,
YOUNG HEARTS FAIL,
ANYTIME,
PRESSURISED,
OVERHEAT,
OVERTIRED
~~ONE~~ ~~TAKE IT~~ TAKE IT
~~NEAT~~, QUICK
~~REL~~ TAKE IT NEAT,
in
~~HOLD~~ YOUR HANDS
WHEN YOU KNEEL
ON ~~YOUR KNEES~~.
CLASP CLASP
YOUR TOUCH YOUR HANDS, TOUCH YOUR FEET

~~ENDLESS~~ HEARTS FAIL,
YOUNG HEARTS FAIL
ANYTIME.
WEARING DOWN,
ON THE RUN
UNDERGROUND,
PUT YOUR HAND

WHERE ITS SAFE.
~~PUT~~ GIVE ME YOUR HAND
~~ONCE MORE PLACE.~~
DO IT AGAIN, + AGAIN.

And she turned to me
with tears in her eyes
and said,
And she 'kicked out,
screaming for her

## GLASS (1978)

Hearts fail, young hearts fail
Any time, pressurised
Overheat, overtired
Take it quick, take it neat
Clasp your hands, touch your feet
Take it quick, take it neat
Take it quick, take it neat

Hearts fail, young hearts fail
Anytime, wearing down
On the run, underground
Put your hand where it's safe
Leave your hand where it's safe

Do it again
Do it again and again and again
Do it again and again and again
Do it again and again and again
Do it again and again and again

Anytime, that's your right
Don't you wish you do it again
Overheat, overtired
Don't you wish you do it again
Don't you wish you do it again
Don't you wish you do it again
Anytime that's your right
Don't you wish you do it again
Anytime that's your right.
Don't you wish you do it again
Don't you wish you do it again
I bet you wish you do it again
Do it again
Do it again
Do it again.

# DISORDER

IVE BEEN WAITING FOR
A GUIDE TO COME +
TAKE ME BY THE HAND,
COULD SENSATION MAKE
ME FEEL THE PLEASURES
OF A NORMAL MAN,
LOSE SENSATION SPARE
THE INSULTS LEAVE THEM
FOR ANOTHER DAY,
BRAND NEW SPIRIT, TOUCH
THESE FEELINGS, TAKE THE
SHOCK AWAY.

ITS GETTING FASTER,
MOVING FASTER. GETTING
OUT OF HAND,
ON THE FOURTH FLOOR
DOWN THE BACKSTAIRS

INTO NO MANS LAND,
LIGHTS ARE FLASHING,
CARS ARE CRASHING
GETTING FREQUENT NOW,
TOUCH THE SPIRIT, TOUCH
THIS FEELING, LET IT
OUT SOMEHOW.

THINKS MORE OF ME,
+ MORE OF US AND WE
WILL MEET AGAIN,
I'M WATCHIN YOU,
WE'RE WATCHIN YOU,
WE TAKE NO PITY FROM
YOUR FRIENDS,
AND WHO IS RIGHT +
WHO CAN TELL +
WHO GIVES A DAMN
RIGHT NOW,
UNTIL THIS FEELING, NEW
SENSATION TAKES HOLD, THEN WE KNOW

DISORDER

## DISORDER (1979)

I've been waiting for a guide to come and take me by the hand
Could these sensations make me feel the pleasures of a normal
    man?
These sensations barely interest me for another day
I've got the spirit, lose the feeling, take the shock away

It's getting faster, moving faster now, it's getting out of hand
On the tenth floor, down the back stairs, it's a no man's land
Lights are flashing, cars are crashing, getting frequent now
I've got the spirit, lose the feeling, let it out somehow

What means to you, what means to me, and we will meet again
I'm watching you, I'm watching her, I'll take no pity from your
    friends
Who is right, who can tell, and who gives a damn right now
Until the spirit new sensation takes hold, then you know
Until the spirit new sensation takes hold, then you know
Until the spirit new sensation takes hold, then you know
I've got the spirit, but lose the feeling
I've got the spirit, but lose the feeling
Feeling, feeling, feeling, feeling, feeling, feeling, feeling.

I walked
grew out
~~L____ lost~~ and I thought
for a time I could see,
~~Never sure~~ No defence ~~In our defence~~ and I thought
for a while you were me,
We were wrong,
In our time,
Always down,
Out of line.

relaxed
I/ ~~collapsed~~ from the day
~~spent~~ filled with bloodsport
in vain,
And returned with the
knowledge that were two the same
Two in Hell.
Two set free,
Too alike,
You to me.

## DAY OF THE LORDS (1979)

This is the room, the start of it all
No portrait so fine, only sheets on the wall
I've seen the nights, filled with bloodsport and pain
And the bodies obtained, the bodied obtained

Where will it end? Where will it end?
Where will it end? Where will it end?

These are your friends from childhood, through youth
Who goaded you on, demanded your proof
Withdrawal pain is hard, it can do you right in
So distorted and thin, distorted and thin

Where will it end? Where will it end?
Where will it end? Where will it end?

This is the car at the edge of the road
There's nothing disturbed, all the windows are closed
I guess you were right, when we talked in the heat
There's no room for the weak, no room for the weak

Where will it end? Where will it end?
Where will it end? Where will it end?

This is the room the start of it all
Through childhood, through youth, I remember it all
Oh, I've seen the nights filled with bloodsport and pain
And the bodies obtained, the bodies obtained, the bodies
  obtained

Where will it end? Where will it end?
Where will it end? Where will it end?

# CANDIDATE

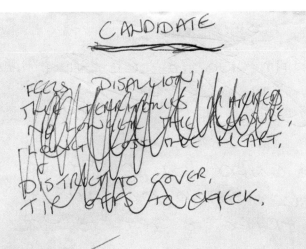

FEELS DISALLION
THE TERRITORIES MARKED
NO LONGER THE PLEASURE,
SINCE LOST THE HEART,
DISTRACT TO COVER,
TIP OFF STAY CHECK.

FORCED BY THE PRESSURE
THE TERRITORIES MARKED
NO LONGER THE PLEASURE,
SINCE LOST THE HEART.

CORRUPTED FROM MEMORY
NO LONGER THE POWER,
CREEPING UP SLOWLY,
THAT LAST FATAL HOUR

I DON'T KNOW WHAT MADE ME,
OR WHAT GAVE ME THE RIGHT,
TO MESS WITH YOUR VALUES,
AND CHANGE WRONG TO RIGHT

PLEASE KEEP YOUR DISTANCE,
THE TRAIL LEADS TO HERE,
BLOOD ON YOUR FINGERS,
BROUGHT ON BY FEAR

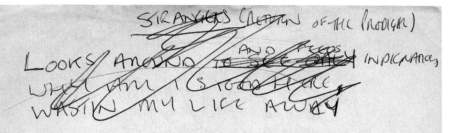

STRAIGHT'S CREATION OF THE (PRODIGAL)
LOOKS AROUND AND FEELS INDIGNANT
WHILE I'M STOOD HERE
WASTIN MY LIFE AWAY

" I CAMPAIGNED FOR NOTHING,
I WORKED HARD FOR THIS,
THEN I TRIED TO GET TO YOU,
YOU TREAT ME LIKE THIS.

JUST SECOND NATURE,
WHAT WE'VE BEEN SHOWN,
WE'RE LIVING BY YOUR RULES,
THEY'RE ALL THAT WE KNOW

see it in front
of your eyes

# CANDIDATE (1979)

Forced by the pressure
The territories marked
No longer the pleasure
Oh, I've since lost the heart

Corrupted from memory
No longer the power
It's creeping up slowly
That last fatal hour

Oh, I don't know what made me
What gave me the right
To mess with your values
And change wrong to right

Please keep your distance
The trail leads to here
There's blood on your fingers
Brought on by fear

I campaigned for nothing
I worked hard for this
I tried to get to you
You treat me like this

It's just second nature
It's what we've been shown
We're living by your rules
That's all that we know

I tried to get to you
I tried to get to you
I tried to get to you
I tried to get to you.

A CHANGE OF SPEED,
A CHANGE TO SLOW DOWN,
A CHANGE OF SCENE,
WITH NO REGRETS,

A CHANCE TO WATCH,
~~TO SEE WHAT WENT WRONG~~,
ADMIRE THE DISTANCE
STILL OCCUPIED,
THOUGH YOU FORGET

DIFFERENT COLOURS, DIFFERENT SHADES,
~~YOU~~ OVERREACHED MISTAKES WERE MADE
DIRECTIONLESS SO PLAIN TO SEE,
A LOADED GUN WON'T SET YOU
FREE.

~~FAILURE TO~~
ROMANCE

## NEW DAWN FADES (1979)

A change of speed, a change of style
A change of scene, with no regrets
A chance to watch, admire the distance
Still occupied, though you forget
Different colours, different shades
Over each mistakes were made
I took the blame
Directionless so plain to see
A loaded gun won't set you free
So you say

We'll share a drink and step outside
An angry voice and one who cried
"We'll give you everything and more
The strain's too much, can't take much more".
Oh, I've walked on water, run through fire
Can't seem to feel it any more
It was me, waiting for me
Hoping for something more
Me, seeing me this time, hoping for something else.

# SHE'S LOST CONTROL

CONFUSION IN HER EYES THAT
SAID IT ALL SHES LOST CONTROL
CLINGING TO THE NEAREST
PASSER BY, SHES LOST CONTROL
AND SHE WASTED ALL THOSE
YEARS IN HER LIFE + SAID IVE
LOST CONTROL AGAIN,
MAYBE A MYTH THAT LEANED AGAINST
HER LIKE A KNIFE, SHES ~~SAID~~
LOST CONTROL AGAIN.


AND SHE TURNED TO ME + TOOK
ME BY THE HAND AND SAID
IVE LOST CONTROL AGAIN,
AND HOW ILL NEVER KNOW JUST
WHY OR UNDERSTAND SHE SAID
IVE LOST CONTROL AGAIN,
+ IN HORROR THAT ONE DAY
I'DEE LEARN THE TRUTH CRIED IVE
LOST CONTROL AGAIN.

# SHE'S LOST CONTROL (1979)

Confusion in her eyes that says it all
She's lost control
And she's clinging to the nearest passer by
She's lost control
And she gave away the secrets of her past
And said I've lost control again
And of a voice that told her when and where to act
She said I've lost control again.

And she turned around and took me by the hand and said
I've lost control again
And how I'll never know just why or understand
She said I've lost control again
And she screamed out kicking on her side and said
I've lost control again
And seized upon the floor, I thought she'd die
She said I've lost control.
She's lost control again
She's lost control
She's lost control again
She's lost control

Well I had to 'phone her friend to state my case
And say she's lost control again
And she showed up all the errors and mistakes
And said I've lost control again
But she expressed herself in many different ways
Until she lost control again
And walked upon the edge of no escape
And laughed I've lost control
She's lost control again
She's lost control
She's lost control again
She's lost control.

TO THE CENTRE OF THE
~~CITY~~ WHERE ALL ROADS
MEET LOOKIN FOR YOU,
TO THE DEPTHS OF THE
OCEAN WHERE ALL HOPE
SUNK SEARCHIN FOR YOU,
MOVING THROUGH THE
SILENCE WITHOUT MOTION
WAITING FOR YOU.
IN A ROOM WITH A
WINDOW IN THE CORNER
~~ONCE WAS~~ TRUTH.

IN THE SHADOW PLAY
ACTIN OUT YOUR OWN DEATH
KNOWING NO MORE.
AS THE ASSASINS ALL
GROUPED IN ~~A~~ FOUR LINES
DANCING ON THE FLOOR,
AND WITH COLD STEEL

ODOUR ON THEIR BODIES
MADE A MOVE TO CONNECT,
AND I COULD ONLY STAND
~~THROUGH ME, IN DISBELIEF~~
AT YOUR NEW GAMES, AS
THE CROWDS ALL LEFT.

I DID EVERYTHING-
EVERYTHING I WANTED TO,
I LET THEM USE USE,
FOR THEIR OWN ENDS.
TO THE CENTRE OF
THE CITIES IN THE
NIGHT LOOKIN FOR YOU.

# SHADOWPLAY (1979)

To the centre of the city where all roads meet, waiting for you
To the depths of the ocean where all hopes sank, searching for you
I was moving through the silence without motion, waiting for you
In a room with a window in the corner I found truth

In the shadowplay, acting out your own death, knowing no more
As the assassins all grouped in four lines, dancing on the floor
And with cold steel, odour on their bodies made a move to
  connect
But I could only stare in disbelief as the crowds all left

I did everything, everything I wanted to
I let them use you for their own ends
To the centre of the city in the night, waiting for you
To the centre of the city in the night, waiting for you.

# INTERZONE

I WALKED THROUGH THE CITY
LIMITS,
  ATTRACTED BY SOME FORCE
WITHIN IT,
  ROUND A CORNER WHERE SOME
PROPHET LAY,
  A WIRE FENCE WHERE
THE CHILDREN PLAYED
  AND I WAS LOOKIN FOR
A FRIEND OF MINE.
  JUST LOOKIN FOR A FRIEND
OF MINE.
        ~~WHEELS~~ CANS SCREECHED HEARD
  ~~THE SOUND OF~~
  CLOUDS ~~OF~~ DUST
  ~~METALLIC BLUE~~
  ~~CHANGING FINISH~~ TURNED
RED WITH RUST,
  IN A GROUP ALL FORGOTTEN

YOUTH,
TURNED ON TO A KNIFE-EDGED
VIEW,
AND I WAS LOOKIN FOR A
FRIEND OF MINE,
YEAH LOOKIN FOR A FRIEND
OF MINE.

DOWN A DARK STREET, HOUSES LOOK THE
SAME, WALKIN ROUND AND ROUND, JUST
TRYIN TO FIND NAMES, TRYIN TO FIND A
CLUE, TRYIN TO FIND A WAY

FOUR × TWELVE WINDOWS TEN
IN A ROW,
LIGHTS SHING ~~AN UNCHANGED~~ LIKE A NEON
~~CLOWS~~, SHOW
NO PLACE TO STOP NO PLACE
TO GO,
I GUESS THEY DIED SOME TIME
AGO,
AND I WAS LOOKING FOR A
FRIEND OF MINE
YEAH LOOKIN FOR A FRIEND
OF MINE.

# INTERZONE (1978)

I walked through the city limits
Someone talked me in to do it
Attracted by some force within it
Had to close my eyes to get close to it
Around a corner where a prophet lay
Saw the place where she'd a room to stay
A wire fence where the children played
Saw the bed where the body lay
And I was looking for a friend of mine
And I had no time to waste
Yeah, looking for some friends of mine

The cars screeched hear the sound on dust
Heard a noise just a car outside
Metallic blue turned red with rust
Pulled in close by the building's side
In a group all forgotten youth
Had to think, collect my senses now
Are turned on to a knife edged view
Find some places where my friends don't know
And I was looking for a friend of mine . . .

Down the dark streets, the houses looked the same
Getting darker now, faces look the same
And I walked round and round
No stomach, torn apart
Nail me to a train, had to think again
Trying to find a clue, trying to find a way to get out!
Trying to move away, had to move away and keep out

Four, twelve windows, ten in a row
Behind a wall, well I looked down low
The lights shined like a neon show
Inserted deep felt a warmer glow
No place to stop, no place to go
No time to lose, had to keep on going
I guess they died some time ago
I guess they died some time ago
And I was looking for a friend of mine . . .

# I REMEMBER NOTHING

VIOLENT UNTHINKING,
GET WEAK ALL THE TIME,
VOICES THAT DRIFT IN
MADE JUST PAST THE TIME,

ME IN MY OWN WORLD,
YOU THERE BESIDE,
THE GAP SO ENORMOUS,
WE STARE FROM EACH SIDE,

VIOLENT MORE VIOLENT,
HIS HAND CRACKS THE CHAIR,
SO MOVES ON REACTION,
THEN SLUMPS IN DESPAIR.

TRAPPED IN A CAGE,
AND SURRENDERS TO SOON,
ME IN MY OWN WORLD,
ONE THAT YOU KNEW,

# I REMEMBER NOTHING (1979)

We were strangers
We were strangers, for way too long, for way too long
We were strangers, for way too long
Violent, violent . . .

Were strangers
Get weak all the time, may just pass the time
Me in my own world, yeah you there beside
The gaps are enormous, we stare from each side
We were strangers for way too long

Violent, more violent, his hand cracks the chair
Moves on reaction, then slumps in despair
Trapped in a cage and surrendered too soon
Me in my own world, the one that you knew
For way too long
We were strangers for way too long
We were strangers
We were strangers for way too long
For way too long.

## TRANSMISSION

RADIO, LIVE TRANSMISSION.
RADIO, LIVE TRANSMISSION,

LISTEN TO THE SILENCE, LET
IT RING ON,
EYES, DARK GREY LENSES
FRIGHTENED OF THE SUN,
WE COULD HAVE A FINE
TIME LIVING IN THE NIGHT,
LEFT TO BLIND DESTRUCTION
WAITING FOR OUR SIGHT.

AND WE WOULD GO ON
AS THOUGH NOTHING
WAS WRONG,
AND HIDE FROM THE
DAYS WE REMAINED
ALL ALONE,

STAYING ~~XXXXX~~ IN THE SAME
PLACE. STARING OUT THE TIME,
TOUCHING FROM A DISTANCE
FURTHER ALL THE TIME.

AND I COULD CALL OUT
WHEN THE GOING GETS
TOUGH,
THE THINGS WE WERE TAUGHT
ARE NO LONGER ENOUGH,
NO LANGUAGE, JUST
SOUND, THATS ALL WE
NEED KNOW,
TO SYNCHRONISE LOVE
TO THE BEAT OF THE
SHOW.

# TRANSMISSION (1978)

Radio, live transmission
Radio, live transmission.

Listen to the silence, let it ring on
Eyes, dark grey lenses frightened of the sun
We would have a fine time living in the night
Left to blind destruction
Waiting for our sight

And we would go on as though nothing was wrong
And hide from these days we remained all alone
Staying in the same place, just staying out the time
Touching from a distance
Further all the time

Dance, dance, dance, dance, dance, to the radio
Dance, dance, dance, dance, dance, to the radio
Dance, dance, dance, dance, dance, to the radio
Dance, dance, dance, dance, dance, to the radio

Well I could call out when the going gets tough
The things that we've learnt are no longer enough
No language, just sound, that's all we need know, to synchronise
    love to the beat of the show

And we could dance

Dance, dance, dance, dance, dance, to the radio
Dance, dance, dance, dance, dance, to the radio
Dance, dance, dance, dance, dance, to the radio
Dance, dance, dance, dance, dance, to the radio.

HERE EVERYTHING IS BY DESIGN,
YOUR HOPES, YOUR DREAMS, YOUR PARADISE,
AND POLITICIANS ONE MORE VICE,
HEROES, IDOLS CRACKED LIKE ICE.

HERE EVERYTHING IS KEPT INSIDE,
SO TAKE A CHANCE + STEP OUTSIDE,
LOSE SOME SLEEP + SAY YOU TRIED,
TO SHOW THE CHOICE~~S~~ ~~THEY OFTEN HIDE~~
THEN STEP OUTSIDE.

WE'RE ~~THE~~ THE PRODUCT, WAY WERE MADE,
PURE FRUSTRATION FACE TO FACE,
A POINT OF VIEW, CREATES MORE WAVES,
THAN BEING TOLD THE TIME + PLACE.

# AUTOSUGGESTION (1979)

Here, here
Everything is by design
Everything is by design

Here, here
Everything is kept inside
So take a chance and step outside
Your hopes, your dreams, your paradise
Heroes, idols cracked like ice.

Here, here
Everything is kept inside
So take a chance and step outside

Pure frustration face to face
A point of view creates more waves
So take a chance and step outside

Take a chance and step outside
Lose some sleep and say you tried
Meet frustration face to face
A point of view creates more waves

So lose some sleep and say you tried
So lose some sleep and say you tried
So lose some sleep and say you tried
So lose some sleep and say you tried

Say you tried
Say you tried
Say you tried
Say you tried . . .

Yeah, lose some sleep and say you tried
Yeah, lose some sleep and say you tried
Yeah, lose some sleep and say you tried
Yeah, lose some sleep and say you tried.

No ~~I DONT KNOW~~

NO     I DON'T KNOW JUST WHY
NO     I DON'T KNOW JUST WHY
WHICH WAY TO TURN
I'VE GOT THIS TICKET TO USE,


THRU CHILDLIKE WAYS REBELLION
AND CRIME,
TO REACH THIS POINT AND RETREAT
BACK AGAIN
THRU BROKEN HEARTS
AND ALL THE WHEELS THAT HAVE
                              TURNED
THE MEMORIES SCARRED + THE
VISION IS BLURRED,


NO     I DON'T KNOW WHICH WAY,
NO     I DON'T KNOW WHICH WAY,
DON'T   KNOW WHICH WAY TO TURN,
THE BEST POSSIBLE USE.

JUST PASSING THRU TILL WHERE
REACH THE NEXT STAGE
BUT ~~WHERE TO GO~~ ~~JUST~~ TO WHERE
WELL, ITS ALL BEEN ARRANGED

JUST PASSING THRU BUT THE
BREAK   MUST BE MADE,
SHOULD WE MOVE ON
OR STAY SAFELY AWAY.

JUST PASSING THRU
TILL WE REACH THE NEXT STAGE,
BUT JUST TO WHERE
I HAD A ~~CHOICE~~
~~BUT IT FEELS~~ ARRANGED
WELL ITS ALL BEEN
JUST PASSING THRU
BUT THE BREAK MUST BE MADE,
FROM ~~SAFELY~~ ON
COULD WE MOVE RELIGION ON,
OR STAY SAFELY AWAY,


THROUGH CHILD~~REN~~ LIKE WAYS,
REBELLION ~~AN~~ AND CRIME,
TO REACH THIS POINT
AND RETREAT BACK AGAIN.
~~THEN WHEELS THAT TURN,~~
~~AN THE MEMORIES SCARRED,~~
~~THE MEMORIES SCARRED~~
~~THE VISION IS BLURRED~~
THE WHEELS THAT HAVE TURNED
AND THE ENERGIES DRAINED,
THE MEMORIES SCARRED
AND THE VISION IS BLURRED


THROUGH CHILDLIKE WAYS
REBELLION + CRIME,
TO REACH THIS POINT + RETREAT
BACK AGAIN,
BROKEN HEARTS
ALL THE WHEELS THAT HAVE TURNED,
THE MEMORIES SCARRED
AND THE VISION IS BLURRED,


OH I DON'T KNOW JUST WHY
NO I DON'T KNOW JUST WHY
WHICH WAY TO TURN
I GOT THIS TICKET TO USE

# FROM SAFETY TO WHERE . . . ? (1979)

No I don't know just why
No I don't know just why
Which way to turn
I got this ticket to use

Through childlike ways rebellion and crime
To reach this point and retreat back again
The broken hearts
All the wheels that have turned
The memories scarred and the vision is blurred

No I don't know which way
Don't know which way to turn
The best possible use

Just passing through, till we reach the next stage
But just to where, well it's all been arranged
Just passing through but the break must be made
Should we move on or stay safely away?

Through childlike ways rebellion and crime
To reach this point and retreat back again
The broken hearts
All the wheels that have turned
The memories scarred and the vision is blurred.

Just passing through, till we reach the next stage
But just to where, well it's all been arranged
Just passing through but the break must be made
Should we move on or stay safely away?

WALK, IN SILENCE,
DON'T WALK AWAY, IN SILENCE,
SEE THE DANGER,
ALWAYS DANGER,
ENDLESS TALKING,
LIFE REBUILDING,
DON'T WALKAWAY, FACE LIKE DANGERS.

~~FEAR~~ + VIOLENCE
DON'T STAY AWAY FROM,
SEE THE DANGER,
ALWAYS DANGER,
RULES ARE BROKEN,
FALSE EMOTIONS,
DON'T WALKAWAY, FACE THE DANGERS

PEOPLE LIKE YOU FIND IT EASY TO FORGET,
ALWAYS IN TUNE,
WALKING ON AIR,
YOU HUNTING IN PACKS BY THE
RIVERS IN THE STREETS,
BUT ITS OVER TOO SOON,
THEN MAYBE YOU'LL CARE,
+WE'LL WALKAWAY, FACE THE DANGER.

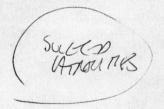

## ATMOSPHERE (1979)

Walk in silence
Don't walk away, in silence
See the danger
Always danger
Endless talking
Life rebuilding
Don't walk away

Walk in silence
Don't turn away, in silence
Your confusion
My illusion
Worn like a mask of self-hate
Confronts and then dies
Don't walk away

People like you find it easy
Naked to see
Walking on air
Hunting by the rivers
Through the streets
Every corner abandoned too soon
Set down with due care
Don't walk away in silence
Don't walk away

DEAD SOULS

SOMEONE TAKE THESE DREAMS AWAY,
THAT POINT~~ING~~ ME TO ANOTHER DAY,
A DUEL OF PERSONALITIES
THAT STRETCH ALL TRUE REALITIES.

WHERE FIGURES FROM THE PAST
STAND TALL,
AND MOCKING TONES RING THROUGH
THE HALLS

~~A~~ IMPERIALISTIC ~~DAYS #S~~ HOUSE OF PRAYER
CONQUISTADORS WHO TOOK THEIR SHARE

~~SOMEONE~~
ANOTHER DAY, ANOTHER TIME,
THESE ~~DREAMS~~ CAN'T STOP OR RECTIFY,
BUT FALL INTO A LIVING SEA,
~~AND I CAN'T~~
~~BUT ~~OBSESSIONS KEEP~~~~
~~BRAINS~~ ME UP, KEEPS CALLING ME ~~ME~~

## DEAD SOULS (1979)

Someone take these dreams away
That point me to another day
A duel of personalities
That stretch all true realities

That keep calling me
They keep calling me
Keep on calling me
They keep calling me

Where figures from the past stand tall
And mocking voices ring the halls
Imperialistic house of prayer
Conquistadors who took their share

That keep calling me
They keep calling me
Keep on calling me
They keep calling me
Calling me, calling me, calling me, calling me
They keep calling me
Keep on calling me
They keep calling me
They keep calling me.

PORTRAYAL OF A NEW
↑
SYSTEMATICALLY DEGRADED,
CAN'T YOU SEE LIFE GETTING HARDER,

SYSTEMATICALLY HES TURNING,
HE FEELS HIS PRIDE STILL BURNING,
CAN'T YOU SEE LIFE GETTING HARDER,
TALKS ME THRU HIS HEARTBREAK,
CRUSHED UNTIL HIS ARMS BREAK,
NO LOVE OR LUST TO TAKE YOU
                         HIGHER.

IVE TAKEN THINGS TO SHOW ME,
EXACTLY WHAT I LIE HERE.
AND
I KNEW MY LIFE IS GETTING HARDER,

# THE SOUND OF MUSIC (1979)

See my true reflection
Cut off my own connections
I can see life getting harder
So sad is this sensation
Reverse the situation
I can't see it getting better

I'll walk you through the heartbreak
Show you all the out takes
I can't see it getting higher
Systematically degraded
Emotionally a scapegoat
I can't see it getting better

Perverse and unrealistic
Try to make it all stick
I can't see it getting better
Hollow now, I'm burned out,
All I need to break out
I can't see life getting higher
Love, life, makes you feel higher
Love, of life, makes you feel higher
Higher, higher, higher, higher
Higher, higher, higher, higher
Love of life, makes you feel higher.

~~UNTIL~~ THE ~~BUTCHER~~

MADE ONE FATAL MISTAKE,
JUST LIKE I DID ONCE BEFORE,
A MUTUAL FEELING TO TAKE,
THE ~~THRILL OF~~ ^ECSTASY^ HAD TURNED SOUR,
PURPOSELY

YEAH JUST ONE FATAL MISTAKE,
CORRUPTION SOILS THE SKIN,
AND THEN THE TRUTH HAD TO BREAK,
SENSED AND SUCKED US ALL IN.

UNTIL THEN JUST ONE MISTAKE.
LIKE I MADE ONCE BEFORE.

JUST ONE FATAL MISTAKE,
WE SAW IT COMING FOR SOME TIME,
~~TURNED~~ ^TILL^ OUR BACKS HAD TO BREAK,
UNDER THE WEIGHT OF THE CRIME

MADE ONE FATAL

# THE ONLY MISTAKE (1979)

Made the fatal mistake
Like I did once before
A tendency just to take
Till the purpose turned sour

Strain, take the strain, these days we love
Strain, take the strain, these days we love

Yeah, the only mistake was that you ran away
Avenues lined with trees, strangled words for the day
Yeah, the only mistake, like I made once before
Yeah, the only mistake, could have made it before

Strain, take the strain, these days we love
Strain, take the strain, these days we love

And the only mistake, led to rumours unfound
Led to pressures unknown, different feelings and sounds
Yeah, the only mistake, like I made once before
Yeah, the only mistake, could have made it before.

# SOMETHING MUST BREAK

TWO WAYS TO CHOSE,
ON A RAZORS EDGE,
REMAIN BEHIND,
OR GO STRAIGHT AHEAD,

ROOMFUL OF PEOPLE, ROOM FOR JUST ONE,
IF I CAN'T BREAK OUT NOW, THE TIME NEVER
COMES

TWO WAYS TO CHOSE,
WHICH WAY TO GO,
DECIDE FOR ME,
PLEASE LET ME KNOW,

WALKED THRU THE MIRROR,
SAW I WAS WRONG,
IF I COULD GET BACK TO,
WHERE I BELONG,

TWO WAYS TO CHOSE
WHICH WAY TO GO,
~~THOUGHT~~ THOUGHT FOR ONE,
DESIGNS FOR BOTH,

IF WE WERE IMMORTAL, WE WERE ~~~~ NOT
THERE, WASHED UP ON THE BEACHES,
~~GOT US CROSSING~~ FOR AIR
STRUGGLING

I SEE YOUR FACE STILL IN MY
WINDOW,
TORMENTS YET CALMS, WON'T
SET ME FREE.

SOMETHING MUST BREAK NOW,
THIS LIFE ISN'T MINE,
SOMETHING MUST ~~WAIT~~ BREAK NOW
~~JUST WAITING~~ WAIT FOR THE TIME
SOMETHING MUST BREAK

## SOMETHING MUST BREAK (1979)

Two ways to choose
On a razor's edge
Remain behind
Go straight ahead

Room full of people, room for just one
If I can't break out now, the time just won't come

Two ways to choose
Which way to go
Decide for me
Please let me know

Looked in the mirror, saw I was wrong
If I could get back to where I belong, where I belong

Two ways to choose
Which way to go
Had thoughts for one
Designs for both

But we were immortal, we were not there
Washed up on the beaches, struggling for air

I see your face still in my window
Torments yet calms, won't set me free
Something must break now
This life isn't mine
Something must break now
Wait for the time
Something must break.

WHEN ROUTINE BITES HARD, AND
AMBITION IS LOW,
AS RESENTMENT SETS IN, AND
Emotions won't GROW,
AND WERE CHANGING TOO FAST,
TAKING OPPOSITE ROADS.

THIS BEDROOMS SO COLD, TURNED
AWAY ON YOUR SIDE,
IS MY TIMING SO FLAWED, ~~our~~ NESPECT HAS WORN DRY
~~THINKS~~ ~~WHY IS~~ THINKS STILL THIN APPEAR,
THAT WEVE KEPT THRU OUR LIVES,

CRY OUT IN YOUR SLEEP, ALL MY
FAILINGS EXPOSED,
TASTE IN MY MOUTH, DESPERATION
TAKES HOLD,
JUST THAT SOMETHING SO GOOD,
CANT FUNCTION NO MORE.

# LOVE WILL TEAR US APART (1980)

When routine bites hard
And ambitions are low
And resentment rides high
But emotions won't grow
And we're changing our ways, taking different roads

Then love, love will tear us apart again
Love, love will tear us apart again

Why is the bedroom so cold?
You've turned away on your side
Is my timing that flawed?
Our respect runs so dry
Yet there's still this appeal that we've kept through our lives

But love, love will tear us apart again
Love, love will tear us apart again

You cry out in your sleep
All my failings exposed
And there's a taste in my mouth
As desperation takes hold
Just that something so good just can't function no more

But love, love will tear us apart again
Love, love will tear us apart again
Love, love will tear us apart again
Love, love will tear us apart again.

# THESE DAYS

THE MORNINGS SEEM COLD ALMOST
OUT OF PLACE,
I SEARCHED HARD FOR YOU AND YOUR
SPECIAL WAYS,
THESE DAYS, THESE DAYS.

I SPENT ALL YOUR TIME, LEARNT A
KILLERS ART,
TOOK THREATS AND ABUSE TILL I
PLAYED THE PART,
CAN YOU STAY, THESE DAYS.

USE OUTWARD DECEPTION TO GET
MY WAY,
USE HEARTBROKEN ROMANCES TO
MAKE IT PAY
THESE DAYS, THESE DAYS

DRIFT THROUGH IT ALL THIS THE
MODERN AGE,
TAKE CARE OF IT ALL NOW THE
DEBTS ARE PAID.
CAN YOU STAY, THESE DAYS

THESE DAYS

## THESE DAYS (1980)

Morning seems strange, almost out of place
Searched hard for you and your special ways
These days, these days

Spent all my time, learnt a killer's art
Took threats and abuse till I'd learned the part.
Can you stay for these days?

These days, these days

Used outward deception to get away
Broken heart romance to make it pay

These days, these days

We'll drift through it all, it's the modern age
Take care of it all now these debts are paid
Can you stay for these days?

# ATROCITY EXHIBITION

ASYLUMS WITH DOORS OPEN WIDE,
WHERE THE PEOPLE HAD PAID TO
SEE INSIDE,
FOR ENTERTAINMENT CONVULSIVE
BEEN TYPISTS                    SAYS TO HIMSELF
BEHIND HIS EYES HE SHOUTS
"I STILL EXIST"

IN ARENAS MADE TO KILL FOR A
                            PRIZE,
WIN A MINUTE MORE ADDED ON YOUR
                            TIME,
AND THE SICKNESS IS DROWNED BY
CRIES FOR MORE,
PRAY TO YOUR GOD TO MAKE IT
QUICK + WATCH HIM FALL.


YOU SEE MASS MURDER ON A SCALE
YOUVE NEVER SEEN,
AND THOSE WHO TRY SO HARD BUT NEVER
CAN SUCCEED,
YOU'LL SEE THE HORRORS OF A
FAR AWAY PLACE,
AND MEET THE ARCHITECTS OF LAW FACE
FACE TO FACE.

SITUATIONS THAT WILL NEVER
                    BE RESOLVED,
FREAKS OF NATURE
                    NEVER SEEN TO
HAVE EVOLVED.
OBSERVERS      OUT OF TOUCH.     MOST OF THE
                                    TIME.
"I LOOK AROUND, I CANT SEE WHO I WAS
                            FINE?

## ATROCITY EXHIBITION (1980)

Asylums with doors open wide
Where people had paid to see inside
For entertainment they watch his body twist
Behind his eyes he says, 'I still exist'

This is the way, step inside
This is the way, step inside . . .

In arenas he kills for a prize
Wins a minute to add to his life
But the sickness is drowned by cries for more
Pray to God, make it quick, watch him fall

This is the way, step inside
This is the way, step inside . . .

This is the way
This is the way
This is the way
This is the way
This is the way, step inside
This is the way, step inside . . .

You'll see the horrors of a faraway place
Meet the architects of law face to face
See mass murder on a scale you've never seen
And all the ones who try hard to succeed

This is the way, step inside
This is the way, step inside . . .

And I picked on the whims of a thousand or more
Still pursuing the path that's been buried for years
All the dead wood from jungles and cities on fire
Can't replace or relate, can't release or repair
Take my hand and I'll show you what was and will be.

ISOLATION

~~IN FEAR~~
                                    EVENING,
IN FEAR EVERY DAY EVERY ~~~~,
HE CALLS HER ALOUD FROM ABOVE,
~~WATCHED~~ ~~SECLUDED + WATCHED~~
~~CALLED AND SECLUDED~~ FOR A REASON
        CAREFULLY WATCHED FOR A REASON
PAINSTAKING DEVOTION + LOVE,

                        self preservation
SURRENDERED TO ~~~~,
FROM ~~FROM~~ OTHERS WHO CARE FOR THEMSELVES
A BLINDNESS THAT TOUCHES
PERFECTION,
    BUT HURTS JUST LIKE ANYTHING
ELSE.    — CHORUS —

" MOTHER I TRY~~ED~~ PLEASE
BELIEVE ME"
    IM DOING THE BEST THAT I
CAN.
                        THE THINGS
    IM ASHAMED OF ~~~~
IVE BEEN PUT THROUGH
    IM ASHAMED OF THE PERSON

I AM.    — CHORUS —
                JUST
BUT IF YOU COULD SEE THE BEAUTY,
THESE THINGS I CAN NEVER DESCRIBE,
THE ~~BRIGHTNESS~~ ~~TO END~~ ~~CONDEMNATION~~
~~THIS IS MY OWN CONSOLATION~~,
THESE PLEASURES  + ~~ONE~~ WAYWARD DISTRACTION
~~COLOUR~~ THIS IS MY ^LUCKY PRIZE

# ISOLATION (1980)

In fear every day, every evening
He calls her aloud from above
Carefully watched for a reason
Painstaking devotion and love
Surrendered to self preservation
From others who care for themselves
A blindness that touches perfection
But hurts just like anything else

Isolation, isolation, isolation,

Mother I tried please believe me
I'm doing the best that I can
I'm ashamed of the things I've been put through
I'm ashamed of the person I am

Isolation, isolation, isolation

But if you could just see the beauty
These things I could never describe
These pleasures a wayward distraction
This is my one lucky prize

Isolation, isolation, isolation, isolation, isolation.

# PASSOVER

THIS IS THE CRISIS I KNEW HAD TO
COME,
DESTROYING THE BALANCE I'D KEPT,
UNSETTLING AND DOUBTING AND
TURNING AROUND,
WONDERING WHAT WILL COME
NEXT,
IS THIS THE ROLE THAT YOU
WANTED TO LIVE.
I WAS FOOLISH TO ASK FOR SO MUCH,
WITHOUT THE PROTECTION AND
IN FANCYS' GUARD.
IT ALL FALLS APART AT FIRST TOUCH.

WATCHING THE ~~REEL~~ HOURS AS ~~THEY~~ THIS
COMES TO A CLOSE,
BRUTALLY TAKING ITS TIME,
~~WONDERING~~ WHO ~~DIE~~ CHANGE FOR NO
REASON AT ALL
ITS HAPPENING ALL . THE TIME,

CAN I GO ON WITH THIS
TRAIN OF EVENTS,
DISTURBING AND PURGING MY
MIND,
OR BACK OUT OF MY DUTIES
WHEN ALL'S SAID AND DONE,
I KNOW THAT I'LL LOSE EVERY TIME.

MOVING ALONG IN OUR GOD GIVEN WAYS,
SAFETY IS SAT BY THE FIRE,
SANCTUARY FROM THESE FEVERISH
SMILES,
LEFT WITH A MARK ON THE DOOR
IS JUST THE GIFT THAT I WANTED
TO GIVE,
FORGIVE AND FORGETS WHAT THEY PREACH
OR PASS THROUGH THE DESERTS +
WASTELANDS ONCE MORE
AND SEE ~~THESE ARE~~ DROWNED
BY THE BEACH.

THIS IS THE CRISIS I

KNEO MAD TO COME,
DESTROYING THE BALANCE
I'D KEPT.
TURNING AROUND TO THE NEXT
SET OF LIVES
WONDERING WHAT WILL
COME NEXT.

## PASSOVER (1980)

This is a crisis I knew had to come
Destroying the balance I'd kept
Doubting, unsettling and turning around
Wondering what will come next.
Is this the role that you wanted to live?
I was foolish to ask for so much
Without the protection and infancy's guard
It all falls apart at first touch

Watching the reel as it comes to a close
Brutally taking its time
People who change for no reason at all
It's happening all of the time.
Can I go on with this train of events?
Disturbing and purging my mind
Back out of my duties, when all's said and done
I know that I'll lose every time

Moving along in our God given ways
Safety is sat by the fire
Sanctuary from these feverish smiles
Left with a mark on the door
Is this the gift that I wanted to give?
Forgive and forget's what they teach
Or pass through the deserts and wastelands once more
And watch as they drop by the beach

This is the crisis I knew had to come
Destroying the balance I'd kept
Turning around to the next set of lives
Wondering what will come next.

A CRY FOR HELP, A HINT OF ANAESTHESIA,
THE SOUND FROM BROKEN HOMES
WE USED TO ALWAYS MEET HERE,
A WORRIED PARENTS GLANCE, A KISS,
A LAST GOODBYE,

A CRY FOR HELP, A HINT OF ANAESTHESIA,
THE SOUND FROM BROKEN HOMES, WE USED
TO ALWAYS MEET HERE,
AS HE LAYS ASLEEP, SHE TAKES
HIM IN HER ARMS,
SOME ~~THINGS~~ I HAVE TO DO, BUT
I DON'T WISH YOU HARM,

A WORRIED PARENTS GLANCE, A KISS,
A LAST GOODBYE,
HANDS HIM
~~HER~~ ~~BAG~~ THE BAG SHE PACKED,
THE TEARS SHE TRIED TO HIDE,
A CRUEL WIND THAT BOWS
DOWN TO OUR LUNACY,
AND LEAVES HIM STANDING
COLD, HERE IN THIS COLONY

## COLONY (1980)

A cry for help, a hint of anaesthesia
The sound from broken homes
We used to always meet here
As he lays asleep, she takes him in her arms
Some things I have to do, but I don't mean you harm

A worried parent's glance, a kiss, a last goodbye
Hands him the bag she packed, the tears she tries to hide
A cruel wind that bows down to our lunacy
And leaves him standing cold here in this colony

I can't see why all these confrontations
I can't see why all these dislocations
No family life, this makes me feel uneasy
Stood alone here in this colony
In this colony, in this colony, in this colony, in this colony

Dear God in his wisdom took you by the hand
God in his wisdom made you understand
God in his wisdom took you by the hand
God in his wisdom made you understand
God in his wisdom took you by the hand
God in his wisdom made you understand
God in his wisdom took you by the hand
God in his wisdom made you understand
In this colony, in this colony, in this colony, in this colony.

A LEGACY , SO FAR REMOVED
ONE DAY WILL BE IMPROVED
ETERNAL RIGHTS ,WE LEFT BEHIND,
WE WERE THE BETTER KIND,
TWO THE SAME , ~~TO~~ SET FREE,TO
I ALWAYS LOOKED TO YOU.

WE FOUGHT FOR GOOD, STOOD
SIDE BY SIDE,
OUR FRIENDSHIP NEVER DIED.
ON STRANGER WAVES , THE LOWS + HIGHS
OUR VISION TOUCHED THE SKY,
~~IMMORTALISTS,~~ WITH ~~POINTS~~ TO PROVE,
~~CREATIVE SOULS,~~ ~~TEARS FOR FEARS TOO SOON~~,
I PUT MY TRUST IN YOU.

A HOUSE SOMEWHERE , ON FOREIGN
                                    SOIL,
WHERE AGEING LOVERS CALL
IS THIS ~~IT~~ YOUR GOAL , ~~SUPPLIED~~ YOUR
FINAL NEEDS
         WHERE DOGS + VULTURES EAT,
         COMMITTED STILL
         ~~SOME TREES~~      I TURNED TO GO
I'D PUT MY TRUST IN YOU.
         ~~SEVERAL LINED OUT~~

# A MEANS TO AN END (1980)

A legacy so far removed
One day will be improved
Eternal rights we left behind
We were the better kind
Two the same, set free too
I always looked to you
I always looked to you
I always looked to you

We fought for good, stood side by side
Our friendship never died
On stranger waves, the lows and highs
Our vision touched the sky
Immortalists with points to prove
I put my trust in you
I put my trust in you
I put my trust in you

A house somewhere on foreign soil
Where ageing lovers call
Is this your goal, your final needs
Where dogs and vultures eat
Committed still I turn to go
I put my trust in you
I put my trust in you
I put my trust in you
I put my trust in you
In you. In you. In you
Put my trust in you, in you.

SO THIS IS PERMANENCE,
LOVES SHATTERED PRIDE,
~~WHAT~~ WHAT ONCE WAS INNOCENCE,
~~IS~~ TURNED ON ITS SIDE,
A ~~CLOUDS~~ CLOUD HANGS OVER ME,
MARKS EVERY MOVE.
DEEP IN THIS MEMORY,
OF WHAT ONCE WAS LOVE.

EXCESSIVE FLASHPOINTS,
BEYOND ANY REACH,
SOLITARY DEMANDS FOR,
ALL I'DE LIKE TO KEEP,
LETS TAKE A RIDE OUT,
~~MY FRIENDS TO THE FLOOR~~
TOO SEE WHAT WE CAN FIND,
A VALUELESS COLLECTION,
OF ~~our~~ HOPES + PAST DESIRES.

NOW THAT I'VE REALISED,
HOW ITS ALL GONE WRONG,
GOT TO FIND SOME THERAPY,
~~FORGET EST~~
~~TALKED~~ TREATMENT LASTS TOO LONG,
DEEP IN THE HEART OT,
WHERE SYMPATHY HELD SWAY,
             GOT TO FIND MY DESTINY
~~LOST THE GOOD PERSON~~
+ ~~MADE THE CHANGE TOO~~
  BEFORE ITS ALL TOO    LATE.

OH HOW I WANTED TO, ~~AND SAY THAT ONE DAYS~~ ME.

~~UNTO TO RESPECT~~

PUT INTO PERSPECTIVE,

JUST ~~FOR ONE~~ MOMENT

OH HOW I REALISED,

HOW I WANTED TIME,

PUT INTO PERSPECTIVE,

ALSO HARD TO FIND,

JUST FOR ONE MOMENT,

THOUGHT I'D ~~FOUND~~ GOT MY WAY,

DESTINY

+ ~~WATCHED~~ IT ~~OUT~~ UNFOLDED AWAY.

~~SO~~ I NEVER REALISED,

THE LENGTHS I'D HAVE TO GO,

ALL THE DARKEST CORNERS OF,

A SENSE I DIDN'T KNOW,

JUST FOR ONE MOMENT,

I HEARD SOME~~BODY~~ CALL,

LOOKED BEYOND THE DAY IN
                         HAND
+ THERE WAS NOTHING THERE +
                    AT ALL.

## TWENTY FOUR HOURS (1980)

So this is permanence, love's shattered pride
What once was innocence, turned on its side
A cloud hangs over me, marks every move
Deep in the memory, of what once was love

Oh how I realised how I wanted time
Put into perspective, tried so hard to find
Just for one moment, thought I'd found my way
Destiny unfolded, I watched it slip away

Excessive flashpoints, beyond all reach
Solitary demands for all I'd like to keep
Let's take a ride out, see what we can find
A valueless collection of hopes and past desires

I never realised the lengths I'd have to go
All the darkest corners of a sense I didn't know
Just for one moment, I heard somebody call
Looked beyond the day in hand, there's nothing there at all

Now that I've realised how it's all gone wrong
Gotta find some therapy, this treatment takes too long
Deep in the heart of where sympathy held sway
Gotta find my destiny, before it gets too late.

PROCESSION MOVES ON, THE SHOOTING
IS OVER,
PRAISING THE GLORY OF HISTORIC DEEDS, _loved ones now gone_
TALKING ALOUD AS THEY SIT ROUND
THEIR TABLES,
SCATTERING FLOWERS, WASHED
DOWN BY THE RAIN.

PLACED BY THE GATE, AT THE FOOT OF
THE GARDEN,
WATCHING THEM PASS LIKE CLOUDS
IN THE SKY,
THEY TO CRY OUT IN THE HEAT OF THE _cried out her name_
MOMENT,
POSSESSED BY A FURY, THAT BURNS
+ ~~ashes~~ FROM INSIDE.

CRY LIKE A CHILD, THOUGH THESE
YEARS MAKE ME OLDER,
WITH CHILDREN MY TIME IS
SO WASTEFULLY SPENT,

A BURDEN TO ~~BARE~~ KEEP, THOUGH
THEIR INNER COMMUNIONS
ACCEPT LIKE A CURSE, AN UNLUCKY
DEAL.

STOOD BY THIS GATE AT THE
FOOT OF VIEW THE GARDEN,
MY ~~WORLD~~ STRETCHES OUT
FROM THE FENCE O THE WALL,
NO WORDS COULD EXPLAIN,
NO ACTIONS DETERMINE,
JUST ~~...~~ WATCHING TO THE ~~LEAVES~~ TREES + THE
LEAVES AS THEY FALL

## THE ETERNAL (1980)

Procession moves on, the shouting is over
Praise to the glory of loved ones now gone
Talking aloud as they sit round their tables
Scattering flowers washed down by the rain
Stood by the gate at the foot of the garden
Watching them pass like clouds in the sky
Try to cry out in the heat of the moment
Possessed by a fury that burns from inside.

Cry like a child, though these years make me older
With children my time is so wastefully spent
A burden to keep, though their inner communion
Accept like a curse an unlucky deal
Played by the gate at the foot of the garden
My view stretches out from the fence to the wall
No words could explain, no actions determine
Just watching the trees and the leaves as they fall.

do do do do | do do | de | do d do | do do |

       V    Λ Λ      V

     down  up up     down.

A Pattern is set a reaction
will start,
complete but rejected
too soon,
Looking ahead in the grip
of each hearp
Bept Nothing will keep
me from you
The pitfalls that lie
every vate
Your shadow that
danced by the side of
the road,
Nothing can keep me
from you.

## KOMAKINO (1980)

This is the hour when the mysteries emerge
A strangeness so hard to reflect
A moment so moving, goes straight to your heart
The vision has never been met
The attraction is held like a weight deep inside
Something I'll never forget

The pattern is set, her reaction will start
Complete but rejected too soon
Looking ahead in the grip of each fear
Recalls the life that we knew
The shadow that stood by the side of the road
Always reminds me of you

How can I find the right way to control
All the conflict inside, all the problems beside
As the questions arise, and the answers don't fit
Into my way of things
Into my way of things.

A WIDER ALLIANCE THAT LEADS
TO NEW ROADS BEYOND THE LIMITS,
HOLDING HANDS, JUMPING OFF
WALLS INTO DARK SECLUSION,
CUT OFF FROM THE MAINSTREAM
OF MOST INTIMATE YEARNINGS,
I LEFT MY HEART SOMEWHERE
ON THE OTHER SIDE, I LEFT
ALL DESIRE FOR GOOD. ~~CLINGING~~
CLINGING TO NAKED THOUGHT,
IMPOSSIBLE TACTICS WORKED OUT
FOR IMPOSSIBLE MEANS. THIS IS
THE FINAL MOMENT OF RESPITE.
THE FINAL PAGE IN THE BOOK.
A BITTER CHALLENGE BETWEEN OLD
+ NEW, WITH ONE LAST WARNING.

I COULD LIVE A LITTLE
                  BETTER.
Was the my ~~such a lie~~
~~in when the darkness closed in~~
~~in couldn't broke down feel~~

# SHE'S LOST CONTROL (12" VERSION)

Confusion in her eyes that says it all
She's lost control
And she's clinging to the nearest passer by
She's lost control
And she gave away the secrets of her past
And said I've lost control again
And of a voice that told her when and where to act
She said I've lost control again.

And she turned to me and took me by the hand and said
I've lost control again
And how I'll never know just why or understand
She said I've lost control again
And she screamed out kicking on her side and said
I've lost control again
And seized up on the floor, I thought she'd die
She said I've lost control again
She's lost control again
She's lost control
She's lost control again
She's lost control

Well I had to 'phone her friend to state her case
And say she's lost control again
And she showed up all the errors and mistakes
And said I've lost control again
But she expressed herself in many different ways
Until she lost control again
And walked upon the edge of no escape
And laughed I've lost control again
She's lost control again
She's lost control
She's lost control again
She's lost control

I could live a little better with the myths and the lies
When the darkness broke in, I just broke down and cried
I could live a little in the wider line
When the change is gone, when the urge is gone
To lose control. When here we come.

# APPENDIX ONE

## EARLY VERSIONS, ALTERNATIVES
## NEW SONGS, PROSE

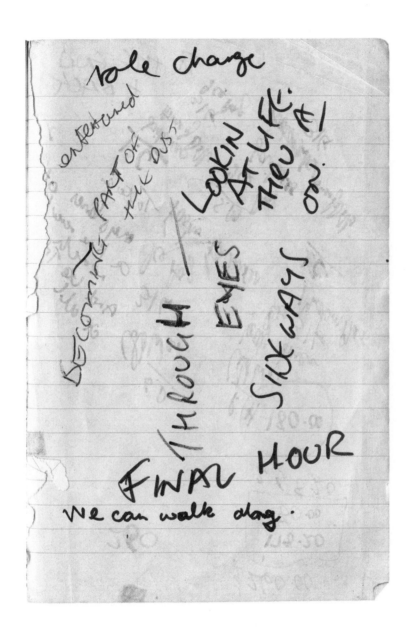

THINK YOUR HAVIN SO MUCH FUN,
STERALISED AT THE AGE OF TWENTY ONE,
THINK THAT YOU'VE GOT IT MADE,
JUST KEEP ON SUCKING TILL YOU GET PAID

THINK YOU KNOW ALL THE RIGHT MOVES,
THINK YOU'VE GOT NOTHIN ELSE TO
PROVE,
SAY YOU'VE SEEN IT ALL ON T.V.
THINK THAT YOU CAN SEE RIGHT
THROUGH ME.

THINK YOU'VE TAKEN ALL THE CHANCES,
THINK YOU KNOW THE LATEST DANCES,
GOD I WISH THAT I WAS YOU,
THEN I COULD BE A NO-ONE TOO.

I used to think there was a God, that in the end everything would be all right, eternal sunshine. Today the sun is shining, everyone says how lovely it is and how were going to have the best summer in years, but I feel sick, were all sick - diseased is a better word to describe our state of mind and body in putting up with the filth around us

I used to dream a lot not so long ago, dream of taking the world, yes you and I we shared a dream together. to take the world and make it ours, shape it as we wanted it. and not give a shit about anyone else. We were legends in our own time but we grew up too soon and our fears took the place of our dreams and reality the place of our tears. We used to walk tall but it all ended too quickly we tossed the dice and it rolled against us.

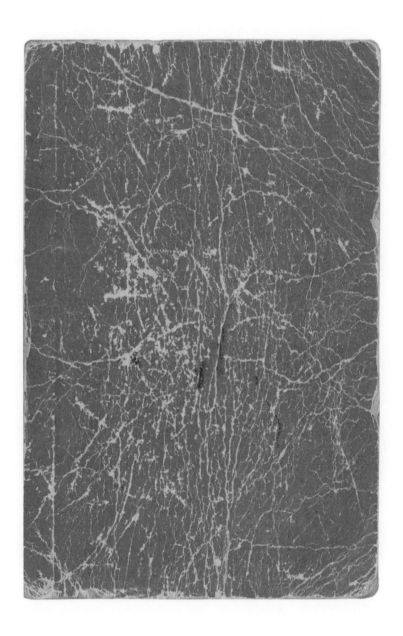

## CONDITIONED

SURE ILL SEE YOU DOWN YOU
DO FOR ME I DID FOR YOU →
YOUR ON THE RIM OF
WHEELS THAT TURN →
YOU'VE LOST YOUR TOUCH :
NOTHING TO BURN.

CURE JUST TAKES YOU
DOWN, WERE DOWN FOR
GOOD THATS UNDERSTOOD —
LIGHTS ON GREEN, ALL
BORROWED TIMES, ITS JUST
THE SAME, A DIFFERENT...
NAME.

CONDITIONED — NO REASON
JUST A WAY OF LIFE.
CONDITIONED — NOT ON
IMPULSE JUST A TRICK
DEVICE

CONDITIONED - MINOR
DETAILS PLANNED FOR EVERY
SPACE.
EVERYTHING TO FIT IN PLACE.

CHANGE IT FROM INSIDE -
IVE LOST YOOR TOUCH IT
DRIVES ME WILD →
IT DRIVES YOU ON
ANOTHER ROOM, THE WAY
THEY LET YOOR MOTHERS
WOMB

JUST WHOS IN THE
CHAIR, TO THINK FOR
ME TO MAKE ME CARE →
TURN DOWN THE SOUND,
TURN DOWN MY PULSE,
CONTROL MY HEART,
THE SOUNDS TOO
MUCH.
IM SO?

CONDITIONED - WHAT A WAY
NO WAYOF LIFE.
CONDITIONED

CONDITIONED - TO THE
WAY YOU WANT MY SAY
CONDITIONED - RELIEFS JUST
SOME SMALL PHASE.

CRIME ~~AGAINST~~ ~~THE~~ ~~INNOCENTS~~

LOCKED AWAY IN IGNORANCE
TRYING TO FIND SOME FUN
IGNORANCE / TRUTH / IGNORANCE.
THE CRIMES HAVE LONG BEGUN

NO REALISATION, IS ~~IT~~ IT
TO MUCH TO TAKE.
AND I REALLY THINK
YOU WENT TOO FAR, NO
SAVIOUR FOR OUR SAKES
ALL TOO YOUNG TO
UNDERSTAND TOO OLD TO
GIVE A ~~FUCK~~,
WHEN YOUR CUTTING
DOWN THE UNDERDOG,
AND BLAMING IT ON
~~FUCK~~.

JUST WATCHIN YOU —
TEARING STRIPS OFF JUST
FOR FUN TO GET A BETTER FIT.
ALL EYES ON YOU — SEX
INDUCED, THE LABOUR PROVE
JUST WATCHIN EVERY DRIP
WAITIN FOR YOU —
BOUGHT US OUT TO CLOSE
ALL DOORS WITH BROKEN LAWS
— YOUR LAWS DON'T FIT.

ITS ALL SO COLDLY LOGICAL
~~THEY SAY~~ WITHOUT A TRACE
OF FEAR.
INTENTIONS, MASK INDEFFER
ENCE, BUILT UP THROUGHOUT THE
YEARS.
NOT TELEVISED, CONCEALS
THE MOTIVES, ~~XXXXXX~~
NOT WAITING TO ADJUST
TO CASE

TILL THE CANCER GROWS,
REPLACING HOPE + YOU ARE
THE DISEASE.
  JUST WATCHIN YOU
  SOME MINOR INCIDENT -
AN INSTANT EYES TURN BLIND
ALL EYES ON YOU -
  JUST SOME KIND OF ACCIDENT
IN GOOD NAME LEFT BEHIND
  WAITIN FOR YOU -
DESTROYING GAINS, ALL
LOST AGAIN, BUT KEPTIN MIND
- YOUR WAY BEHIND.

SOME STRANGER ATROCITY
COMMITT IN SILENCE NOW,
NOT IN THESE TIMES.
ANOTHER WORLD, BUT
ITS SO CLOSE SOMEHOW

A NEWS, FOR
THOSE WHO SERVE
THE LOST ITS WAY,
IN STREETS OF FEAR
AND ALL THOSE HERE
THE INTURNEE OF HATE.

  JUST WATCHIN YOU -
TEARING STRIPS OFF JUST
FOR FUN TO GET A
BETTER FIT,
ALL EYES ON YOU -
BROKEN CAUSE NO ONE
KNOWS THE REAL CAUSE,
WERE IT.
  WAITIN FOR YOU -
ULTIMATUM CHANGE IT
SOON DON'T CLING TO EVERY
BIT
  - IT JUST WON'T FIT.

## OUT OF TOUCH

ON THE WASTELINE,
HEARTBREAK MAINLINE,
IN A HURRY, TO GET SOMEWHERE
DIVORCED FROM WHAT'S
REAL SO EARLY.
ALL A WASTE OF NOTHING
REALLY.
ARRIVE TOO LATE — DON'T
YOU KNOW YOUR OUT OF TOUCH

PASS THE DATELINE
ALL ON YOUR TIME.
IN A HURRY, TO GET
SOMETHING,
STARIN AT YOUR OWN
TWO FACES,
FEEDIN OFF YOUR
PRIVATE CRAZES.
YOUR OUT ON YOUR OWN
— OUT — OUT OF TOUCH

NERVOUS FEELING,
NO SCENE STEALING,
CAN YOU REACH THE
OUTER LIMITS.
STUCK INSIDE YOUR
PEN TOO LONG.
FORGOTTON MOVES
WHERE YOU WENT
WRONG
— YOU'VE LOST THE
FEELING, NOW YOUR
OUT OF TOUCH.

EMPTY STATION
TOO LONG WAITIN,
IN A HURRY TO GET SOMEWHERE
DIVORCED FROM
PROMISE FOR EVERYTHING SO EARLY
ALL A WASTE OF NOTHING
REALLY
YOU WERE NEVER THERE
ALWAYS OUT OF TOUCH

THE LEADERS OF MEN.
BORN ~~OUT OF~~ ~~HERE~~ ~~ONCE~~
~~OF OUT~~ YOUR FRUSTRATION
~~GOOD~~ ~~INTENTIONS~~
LEADERS OF MEN,
JUST A STRANGE INFATUATION

LEADERS OF MEN,
MADE A PROMISE FOR A NEW
LIFE

LEADERS OF MEN
MADE A VICTIM OUT OF
YOUR LIFE –

INTRO
VERSE
~~KEY~~ CHORUS
VERSE
KEY CHANGE
VERSE
QUIET
VERSE
FINISH

(WAITING FOR THE)

~~HERE COMES~~ ICE AGE

SCRATCHING OUT ATROCITY,
SPLINTERED IN THE SAND,
IN A DEATHSHROUD LOOKING
BACK,
    WALKING HAND IN HAND.
DRAW THE LINES ONTO YOUR
FACE,
    TO MAKE IT LOOK BRAND NEW,
NOTHING HERE WILL FIT
IN PLACE,
    TO SCREEN THE LIKES OF YOU.

STRANDED IN HOSTILITY,
BURIED FURTHER DOWN,
                  CHURCHYARD
WAITING IN A CONVENT.
FOR THE SONS TO COME AROUND,
    BURNING DOWN CONVENTIONS
NOW,

TO GIVE ME ALL THE PROOF,
NOTHING HERE WILL HOLD
SOMEHOW, GLIMPSE
TO GIVE A HINT OF TRUTH.

I'LL WAIT FOR A PROMISE.
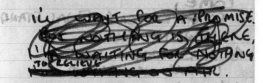
SEARCHING FOR SOME
OTHER LIFE.
TO HIDE BEHIND YOUR DOOR
ON A STRANGE WAVE PLUNGING
DOWN.
WITH HOPES FOR LITTLE MORE.
SOMEONE MIGHT HAVE
CHANGED SOMEWHERE.
TO BRING US INTO LINE.
ALL SO NEAR TO HIT

AND RUN,
TO CUT THE GAPS IN TIME.

WAITING FOR THE COLD TO
COME,
TO MAKE ONE FINAL STAND
VIEWING SCENES IN
BLACK AND WHITE,
WALKING HAND IN
HAND
REACHING FROM THE
DISTANCE,
TO FIND SOME STRENGTH
AGAIN.

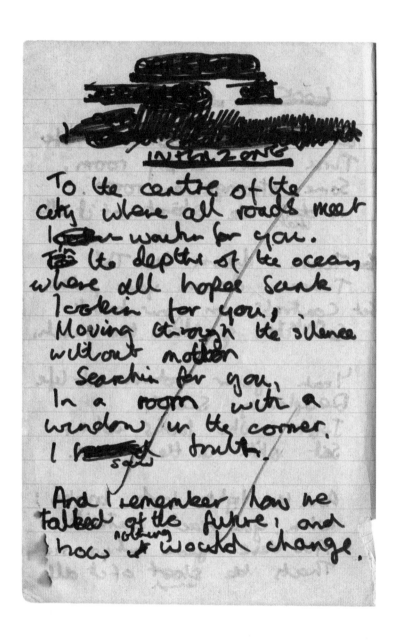

To the centre of the
city where all roads meet
I ~~will~~ wait for you.
~~To~~ the depths of the ocean
where all hopes sank
I ~~lookin~~ for you,
Moving through the silence
without ~~motion~~
    Searchin for you,
In a room with a
window in the corner.
I ~~saw~~ truth.

And I remember how we
talked of the future, and
how nothing it would change.

And how the past no matter
how bad, must always remain
And in the night, when sleep
they took you ~~~~~~
Nothing was said,
And how I wished in the
morning that it was me
who was Taken instead

I CAN SEE A THOUSAND
WILLS JUST BENDING IN
THE NIGHT,
AND ALL THE PRETTY
FACES PAINTED GREY TO
MATCH THE SKY,
AND FROM THESE THINGS
WE SEE AN ~~~~~ NEVER
SEEN BEFORE,
A PICTURE IN MY MIND
OF WHATS TO COME BEFORE
THE STORM.

IN TIME.
DESTROY GOD.
IN YOUR LIFETIME.

He desires love,
In some special way,
~~Against all~~ perception
Fed with ~~gold~~ ~~slender~~ ~~cruelly~~
~~Lover~~ pearls of decay. ~~past~~
He remember,
How to guilty have seen,
The pure but selfish,
Buried deep in his dreams,

He sees, a vision in the sky
Lookin down at him,
Callen him by name
Yeah he ~~sees~~ ~~too them~~
sky, ~~starin down at him~~ ~~of what night have been~~
But the past must still remain

He desires love
In some perfect affair,
In hotels of steel and glass,
Just to cross on the stairs,

But he can still see;
All the angels in ~~~~ time
~~~~ not defined,
As his dreams of ecstasy
Turned to nightmares A crime.

He sees a vision in the sky,
Lookin down at him,
How the past will still remain
Yeah he sees a vision in the
sky, starin down at him
~~They'll~~ always see the same

Sure it'll see you down
You do for me I did for you,
Cure just takes you down
were down for good thats
understood.

Just washed up on the shore
Picture in my mind of what
to come before the storm.
In Time, We don't belong
In Our own Lifetime.

I can feel an emptiness
and see hands held in shame,
Trapped inside a legacy
of everyone to blame.
In the distance see myself just
washed up on the shore,
A picture in my mind of
what will come before the
storm
In Time, We don't belong, to
our own lifetime.

We wont crawl and never show
                    our faces,
we'll stand firm and never
show the traces,

I can see a thousand wills
just bending in the night.
And all the pretty faces
painted grey to match the sky,
From a distance seeing
friends just washed up on to shore,
A picture in my mind of
whats to come before the storm,

~~In time,~~ In time, we don't
~~Betraying love~~ in our own
In your own ~~lifetime~~ lifetime.

fear ~~re~~
I can ~~hear~~ voices lost in
echoes as they build,
New homes to hide the
sadness that the search for ~~no~~ more
~~black~~ killed,
From a by road seeing friends

of the fear we knew.
but allways could disguise,
of this sinking feeling hid
behind our eyes

We have passed thru the
~~stages~~ stages,
And more our heads "in
inward gazes,—
To see in.
To a life that won't begin.

You've tried so many different
ways
TO reach the end of all
your problems,
Always looking to
get caught,
And never once would
give a thought.
To those in closed condition

Conditions of a captive
soul

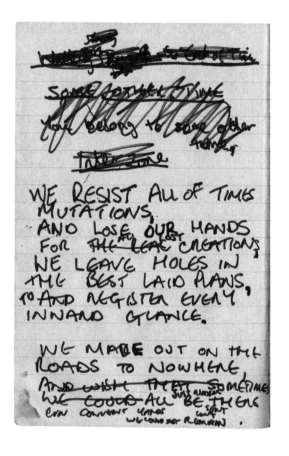

~~Some other time~~

~~You belong to some other~~

~~Intertwine~~

WE RESIST ALL OF TIMES
MUTATIONS,
AND LOSE OUR HANDS
FOR ~~THE LAST~~ CREATIONS
WE LEAVE HOLES IN
THE BEST LAID PLANS,
TO AND REGISTER EVERY
INNARD GLANCE.

WE MADE OUT ON THE
ROADS TO NOWHERE,
~~AND WISH THAT~~ SOMETIME
~~WE COULD~~ ALL BE THERE
ON CONVENT HANDS
WE COULD ALL REMAIN.

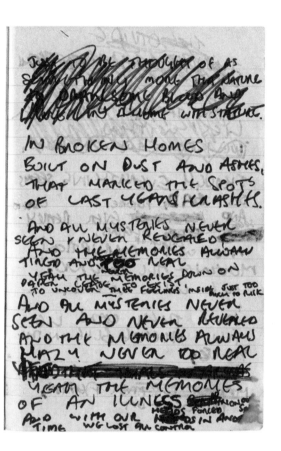

IN BROKEN HOMES
BUILT ON DUST AND ASHES,
THAT MARKED THE SPOTS
OF LAST YEARS FLASHES.

AND ALL MYSTERIES NEVER
SEEN & NEVER REVEALED
AND THE MEMORIES ALWAYS
TINGED AND TOO REAL
YEAH THE MEMORIES DOWN ON
PAPER CREATED TO UNCOVER THESE FEELINGS INSIDE
AND ALL MYSTERIES NEVER
SEEN AND NEVER REVEALED
AND THE MEMORIES ALWAYS
HAZY NEVER TOO REAL
YEAH THE MEMORIES
OF AN ILLNESS
AND WITH OUR HEADS FORCED SO
TIME WE LOST ALL CONTROL

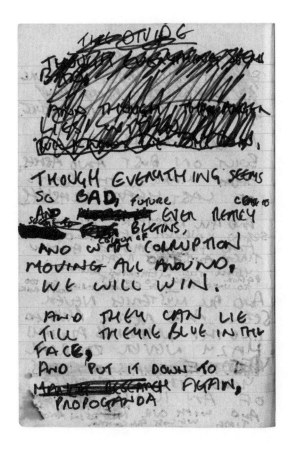

THE GIVING

THOUGH EVERYTHING SEEMS
SO BAD, FUTURE COMING
AND ~~SEEM TO~~ EVER REALLY
BEGINS,
AND WITH CORRUPTION
MOVING ALL AROUND,
WE WILL WIN.

AND THEY CAN LIE
TILL THEY'RE BLUE IN THE
FACE,
AND PUT IT DOWN TO
~~MATTER TOGETHER~~ AGAIN,
PROPOGANDA

THOUGH THE HEARTBREAK
WILL NEVER BE ERASED
WE WILL WIN.

AND THOUGH EVERYTHING
AGAINST US AT THE
START,
THERE'S A STRANGE HOLD
BURNING DEEP WITHIN,
AND CONVERSATION ALWAYS
KEEPS US APART
WE WILL WIN.

# INTERZONE

I walked through the
city limits,
~~Attracted~~ by some force
within it,
Round a corner ~~they~~
~~by~~ where ~~a~~ _some phosphor_
lay, A ~~wire~~ level where
~~Through as each~~ where
the children played.
I was ~~looking~~ for a
friend of mine, _looking_
Just ~~an~~ ~~a dead~~ old friend
of mine.

WHEELS SCRATCHED
~~Bycle~~ ~~row~~ _a_ sound on dust,
~~In a hurry to the his~~
~~house of bay~~ + METALIC FINISH QUICKLY
In a group, _all_ forgotten
youth,

Turned on to a knife
edge view.
And I was ~~looking~~
~~was~~ lookin for a friend of
mine
yeah ~~lookin~~ lookin for mo
friend of mine

~~2x12~~ SMALL WINDOWS ~~2x12 FOR~~
IN A ROW,
ELECTRIC LIGHTS WITH
UNEARTHLY GLOW,

## END OF TIME

WE RESIST ALL OF
TIMES MUTATIONS,
AND LOSE OUR HANDS
FOR ALL LOST CREATIONS
WE LEAVE HOLES IN
THE BEST LAID PLANS,
AND REGISTERED EVERY
INWARD GLANCE.

FOR ALL MYSTERIES
NEVER SEEN + NEVER
REVEALED,
AND THE MEMORIES
ALWAYS TIMED AND
NEVER TOO REAL,
YEAH THE MEMORIES
DOWN ON PAPER CEASE TO EXIST
TO UNCOVER ALL TRUE
FEELINGS INSIDE JUST TOO
MUCH TO RISK.

WE MADE OUT DOWN
THE ROADS TO NOWHERE,
AND ~~REALLY~~ LOST ALL
PURPOSE IN THE RUSH TO GET THERE
FROM BROKEN HOMES
BUILT ON DUST + ASHES,
THAT MARKED THE
SPOTS OF LAST YEARS CRASHES

FOR ALL MYSTERIES N EVER
SEEN + NEVER REVEALED.
AND THE MEMORIES ALWAYS
HAZY N EVER TOO REAL
YEAH THE MEMORIES OF A
FUTURE EVERYONE SHARED,
SO WHEN THE TIME CAME,
LOOKING OVER OUR SHOULDERS
NOBODY CARED,

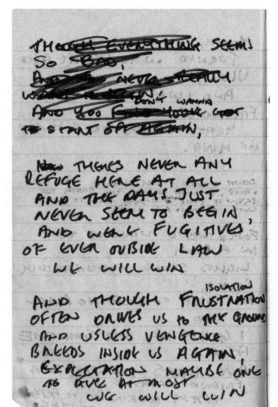

~~THOUGH EVERYTHING SEEMS~~
~~SO BAD,~~
~~AND SO NEVER REALLY~~
~~WORTH~~ DON'T WANNA
~~AND YOU~~ ~~HAVE~~ GOT
TO START OFF ~~AGAIN~~,

~~NOW~~ THERES NEVER ANY
REFUGE HERE AT ALL
AND THE DAYS JUST
NEVER SEEM TO BEGIN
AND WE'RE FUGITIVES,
OF EVER OUTSIDE LAW
WE WILL WIN
                    ISOLATION
AND THOUGH FRUSTRATION
OFTEN DRIVES US TO THE GROUND
AND USLESS VENGENCE
BREEDS INSIDE US AGAIN
EXPECTATION MAYBE ONE
~~TO GIVE AT MOST~~
WE WILL WIN

YEAH CONVENTION ALWAYS
KEEPS US APART,
IVE SEEN THE SOULOF
OF CONVENTION ~~HOW~~ WITHIN,
AND THEY CAN LIE TILL
RUSHER BLUE IN THE FACE
WE WILL WIN

JUST AT THE CASK STANDING
HERE AU CUT FORIGO

I walked
I ~~lost~~ and I thought
for a time I could see;
~~in~~ ~~can't defeat~~ and I thought
for a while you were me,
We were wrong,
In our time,
Always down,
Out of line.

I /relaxed ~~compared~~ from the days
~~spent~~ filled with bloodsport
in vain,
And returned with the
Knowledge that were two to same
Two in Hell.
Two set free,
Too alike,
You to me.

And /after watched
everything pass us by in due
course,
Always /tied by a mutual
feeling that lost,
We were two,
Two in hell
Two set free
Known to hell,

I'm used to nothing
No gains to me,
My only reasons the
things that I see,
Down on the sidewalk
she's so hungry & cold,
but she can't buy
nothin' cause she's already
been sold.

Don't talk of menaces,
Spare me ~~no~~ thought,
No ~~[crossed out]~~ lawyers
hold my own courts,
And I'll be waitin'
when you get down
the stairs
You took the role and
now you'll pay for
the fair,
~~[crossed out]~~

and I thought for a time
I was lost for a time
~~and~~ I thought I could see
I was ~~[crossed out]~~ lost for a time
and I thought you were
me.
We we wrong,
In our time.
We were out,
out of line.

I was ~~lost~~ and the days
filled with blood spots in
vain.
I was lost but I knew
then that were two the same
Two in hell,
Two set free,
Too alike,
You to me.

I never used to worry
too much,
We Were well prepared,
We lived in ~~prepared~~
used apartments,
And used de walls for
stairs.

Don't lean on me,
Don't get me wrong,
~~We~~ played along,
Til I could see.

NOVELTY.
WAVES ?
~~LEAVING SIEGE~~ INTER
.ZONE
AT A LATER DATE.
INSIDE THE LINE.
WARSAW
LEADERS OF MEN.
END OF TIME.
ICE AGE !
FAILURES.
NO LOVE LOST &
"REACTION".
DAY OF THE LORDS
WIN
WARZONE
PICTURES
VISIONS

THOUGH YOU FORGOTTEN
EVERYTHING YOU DID BEFORE.
AND THE DAYS NEVER
SEEM TO BEGIN.
AND WITH THE COLOUR OF
CORRUPTION ALL AROUND
WE WILL WIN.

                    FRUSTRATION
AND THOUGH ISOLATION
OFTEN TAKES US TO THE FLOOR
USELESS VIOLENCE BREEDS
WITHIN US AGAIN,
EXPECTATION MAYBE
ONE TO TWO AT MOST
     WE WILL WIN

AND THOUGH CONVENTION
ALWAYS KEEPS US APART,
                    WITHIN,
AND WITH THE COLOUR OF CORRUPTION
                           ALL AROUND

AND THOUGH THERES
NEVER EVER NOTHING
TO SAY,
THERES A STRANGE HOLD
KEEPING US WITHIN,
SO IF CONVENTION ALWAYS
KEEPS US APART
    WE WILL WIN

THOUGH THERES NEVER
ANY REFUGE HERE AT ALL,
AND THE DAYS JUST NEVER
SEEM TO BEGIN,
AND WERE FUGITIVES OF
EVERY LAW,
        OUTSIDE  WE WILL WIN.

SAY THEYLL BE A
CHOSEN FEW,
TUNNELS BURIED IN
THE SAND,
WHILE WE WERE LOOKIN HARD
LOOKIN BACK
WALKIN HAND IN HAND

WE THOUGHT WE DIED IN
AFRICA,
MEMORIES BURIED IN THE
SAND,
IN A DEATHSHROUD LOOKIN
BACK
WALKIN HAND IN
HAND

WE THOUGHT WE DIED
IN ~~ATOZA~~ KOREA

SAVE THE LIVES OF
A CHOSEN ~~FEW~~,
IN TUNNELS DEEP IN
~~████████~~ burit in the sand
An
WALKIN HAND IN
HAND.

mysteries of life never
to reach.
And the tricks in a
kind arena
And the memories
of what would say
And with his hand on the button.
We could walk through
all minds conditions,
And wear the colours of mans
corruption,
And take the road out
best.
We resent all the real corruption

we believe in the elements
of life.
We believe the
mystery of being
seeing

treatment when they put the
blame on you,
I know now just where I
stand these thoughts will
never cross
Victim of security hoping
to get lost.

Bet youre washed the
whole machine
And never missed out
much
Still starin in the mirror
trying so hard not to push
Put you on an wooden
cross nailed reasons to your
hands
Covered in Self Pity now
understand

to searchin for some other
way
To bring some small relief,
Never to be satisfied
And snatch at all beliefs

Didn't have the energy to
make up for my part,
Everything seemed easy but
I didn't have the heart
Things that on the surface
seemed so very much the same
But once you've made the
more. [crossed out] nothing else
remains.

So a[crossed out] afraid to make a
break for fear of what
I'd do,
It can cause repressive

737-5438

We won't forget you,
on Day of the Lords,
when our hearts stopped
when we pull up the
boards,
To relax from,
all the sickness of words,
To escape from,
the collapse of our world

We won't forget you,
When your takin your
share,
of the [crossed out] future
that nobody shared,
when your [illegible] late,
And how the priests queued
in a theatre alone!
To escape from

In the shadow plays acting
out your own death
Knowing no more,
And with cold steel
odour on their bodies
as they walked through the door

As the assasins with the
blood stained collars took
the floor.
And with cold steel
odour on their bodies
made a sign with their eyes,

I can hear the voices lost
in echoes

And the wood
Wife's wood
~~lookd~~ Day of the Lords

In a hotel by the river,
where all thoughts free,
~~Were talked of.~~
And now.

And ~~as they~~ came through
~~the door~~ to
I felt no stone.

And in the room as
they came to take you
I stood still.

And in the night
when they came

And I wondered

I could dream a thousand
dreams to get me thru the
day.

I can feel an emptiness
and see heads held in shame
And visions of a convent
yard with every one
to blame
Sober Picture in my eyes
can take me back to
life before,

We won't forget you,
When you talked of all
love,
In the ~~real courts~~ wheels turned in
the theatre above,
To escape from all the
rumours you'd heard.

I can see     A Picture
             inspired
Things       of what we
             Now know goes
             before

I can ~~see~~ a thousand
wills just bending in
the night
And all the pretty
faces painted grey,
to match the sky,
~~That~~ than soon 'enough
to take me back and life
as before.
And I can feel the

I can hear the voices
~~calling~~ ~~beating~~ to be hear
lost in echoes
~~during the stairs~~ the grace
~~To dream~~ up new solutions
disappearing without trace.

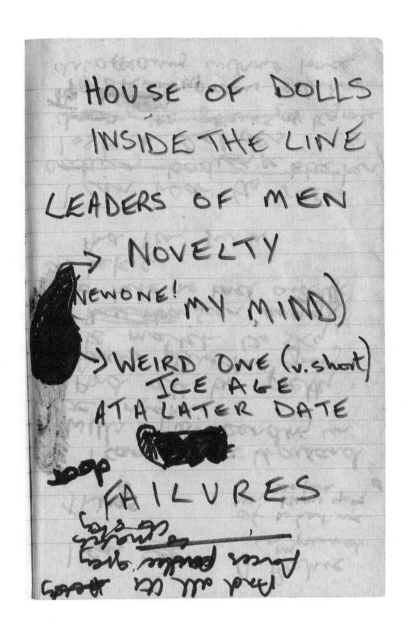

We move silently
you don't check faces
we know are right now

Now I'm feeling silence
like I've never felt before,

In my mind just
take me down to this before,
Now I'm feeling silence like
I've never felt before,

For some the

Peace of mind.

thing Never Mind
I could hear

---

We move on so
silently never checking
faces,
To life some asylum.
and

We move on so silently
Never checks new faces,
Sideways on we're
seeing things in new
light than before,
Sideways on we never
clicked at all.

---

We See things

To live in some asylum
maybe plan some gift
for life.

Wishful Dreaming
Sideways on we're
seeing things never seen
before,

I could See

---

Sure I'll see you
drown yove do
for me i did for you
cure just takes
you down were
down too good
Utah understood,
Conditioned - now were
seeing things were
never seen before
Conditions - no we
never clicked at all
no way out at all

Just whos in the
chair to thank for
me to make me care.

Ragged inside
a legacy

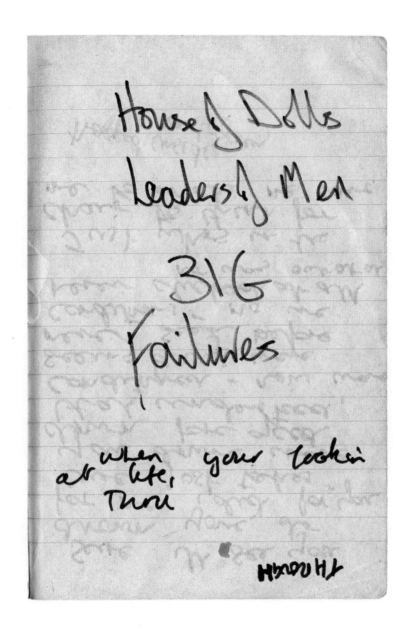

House of Dolls
Leaders of Men
BIG
Failures

at when your lookin
life,
Thru

THROUGH

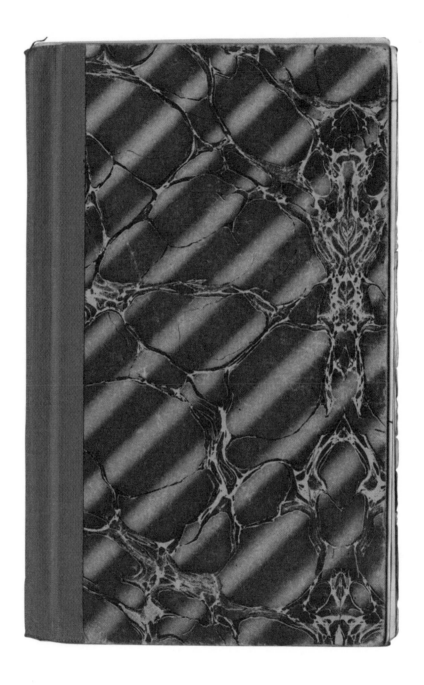

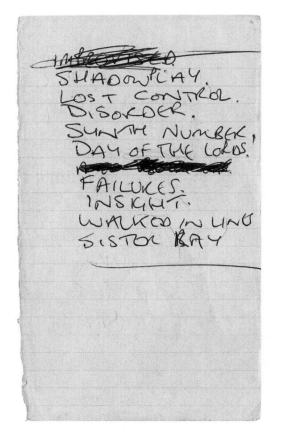

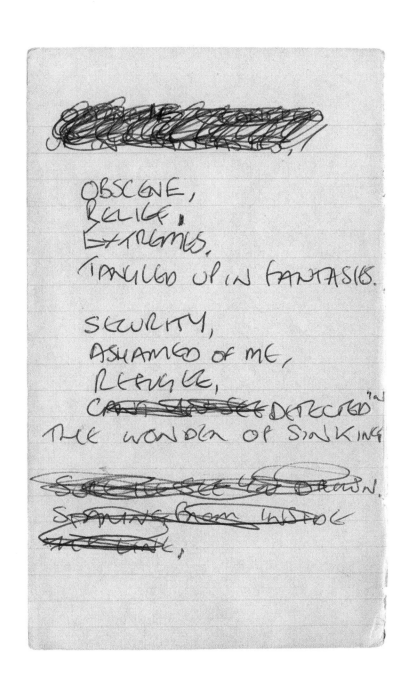

OBSCENE,
RELIEF,
EXTREMES,
TANGLED UP IN FANTASIES.

SECURITY,
ASHAMED OF ME,
REFUGE,
~~CAN SHE SEE~~ DETECTED "IN
THE WONDER OF SINKING

~~SO I CAN SEE YOU~~ DROWN.
~~SPANING~~ FROM INSIDE
~~THE DARK~~,

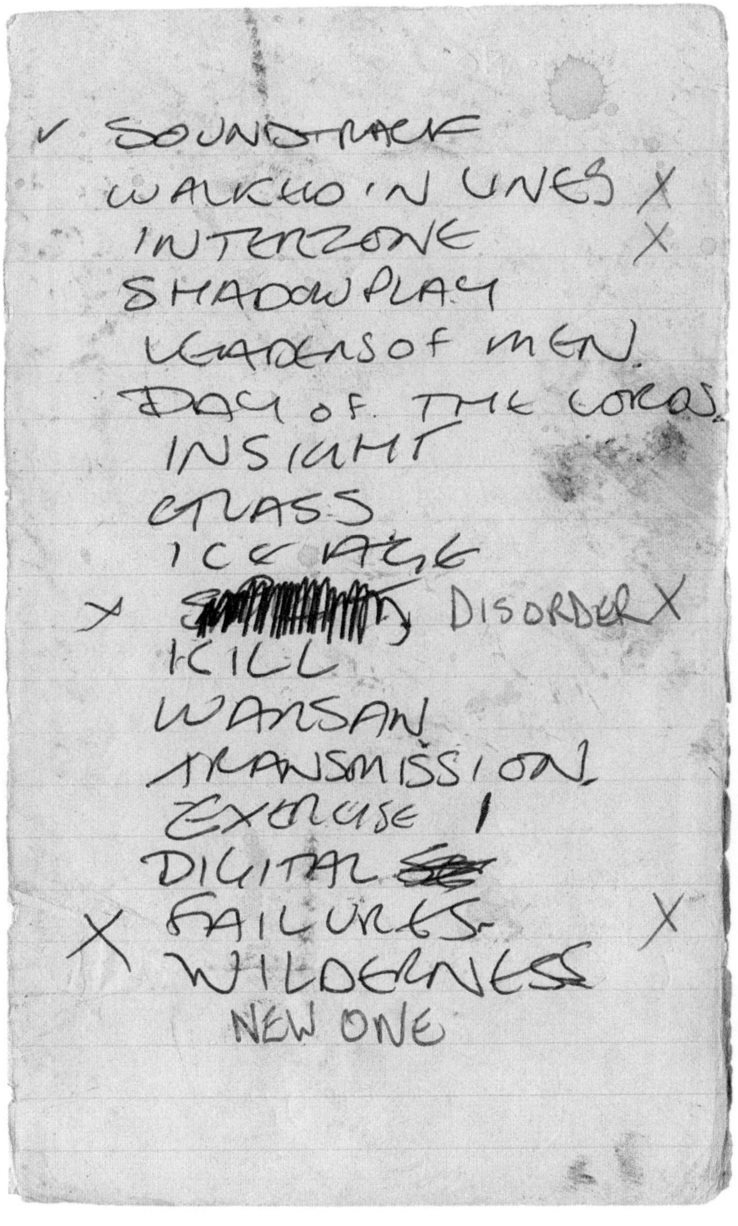

✓ SOUNDTRACK
WALKED IN LINES X
INTERZONE          X
SHADOWPLAY
LEADERS OF MEN
DAY OF THE LORDS
INSIGHT
GLASS
ICE AGE
X ~~████████~~ DISORDER X
KILL
WARSAW
TRANSMISSION
EXERCISE 1
DIGITAL ~~SE~~
X FAILURES          X
WILDERNESS
NEW ONE

TWO ~~SECS~~ MINUTES LATER
THIS ALL TOO MUCH
(REHEARSE)

PUT YOUR HAND,
OUT THE

PUT YOUR HANDS fully saloon
UNTIL IT IS SAFE
DO IT AGAIN.

PROBABLY WEARING FRENCH THIN
AND YET,
YOU WILL WAIT

Splintered
there together scraps for fare.
can't account for autumnace

Trenches
Distance

Behind us

Leeway (to sheel)ne behind
us,

## DEADLINE

DESTINATIONS ALWAYS CHANGE
IT COULD BE HOURS IT
SEEMS LIKE DAYS,
WAIT AROUND AS THOUGH
NOTHINGS CHANGE,
BUT HEAVEN KNOWS WE'VE
TRIED SO LONG
  TO DO
    THE FINAL BREAKTHROUGH

A CHOICE OF GIFTS
WITH HANDS TO DEAL
A NARROW TABLE
~~MADE~~ LEGS OF STEEL,
A WINDOW SEAT WITH
VIEWS THE SAME,
ALL DOWN THE LINE WE
PLAY THE GAME
FOR TWO, NOW WE DREAMED

DESTINATIONS NEVER
CHANGE,
IT SEEMS AS THOUGH
WE'RE DAYS AWAY
AND ALL THE POINTS
THAT LEAD US TO
WE'VE NEVER STOP ASK
PASS ON THEM
AGAIN      DO IT AGAIN

CONFUSION IN HER EYES THAT
SAID IT ALL. LOST CONTROL
CLUTCHING AT THE NEAREST
PASSERBY, LOST CONTROL
AND SHE GAVE AWAY
THE SECRETS OF HER PAST,
AND SAID IVE LOST CONTROL
AGAIN.
AND OF A VOICE THAT
TOLD HER WHEN AND
WHERE TO ACT, SHES
LOST CONTROL AGAIN.

AND SHE TURNED TO ME
AND TOOK ME BY THE
HAND AND SAID, IVE
LOST CONTROL AGAIN.
AND HOW ILL NEVER
UNDERSTAND OR KNOW

JUST WHY, SHES
LOST CONTROL AGAIN
AND SHE KICKED OUT
SCREAMING ON HER SIDE,
AND SAID IVE LOST
CONTROL AGAIN,
AND SEIZED UP ON
THE FLOOR I THOUGHT
SHED DIED,
LOST CONTROL

THERE WERE A THOUSAND REASONS
AND
EXPRESSION IS SO EASY
DONT YOU KNOW FOR
THOSE WHO DONT FEEL
TAKE A CHANCE, JUST
PICK A CARD AND TAKE
YOUR CHANCE, NO PATTERNS

~~Iffrozers~~

Moving on out in a new
~~scene~~ line,
Setting our course by the
sun,
  Leaving the shoreline behind
us,
  We're ~~drifting~~ drifting
apart while we run

SONS CLEFT
I wonder why,
I just can't
see,

  Wheels are in motion
above us,
  Metal + power in
disguise,
  Scared of the danger
around us,   We're
        drowning in
        our paradise
Is even closer,

Wreckage and ~~gold~~ on
the sea bed,
Souls we could never
reclaim,
Grey are the skies that
surround us,
Forcing us farther away.

Moving on out in a
new line,
Setting our course by
the sun,
Leaving it all way behind us
We're drifting apart as
we run

A SHORT WALK.
EVERYTHING I'VE
EVER KNOWN,
SEEN IN THE LIGHT
OF DAY,
I REMEMBER NOTHING.

WHAT WERE TAUGHT,
EXTENSIONS OF ANOTHER
MIND,
IDEAS OF A DIFFERENT
KIND,
I REMEMBER NOTHING

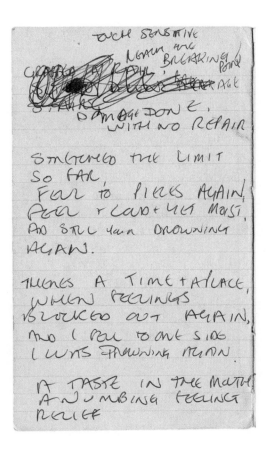

STRUGGLED TO FAR,
 MUTUAL FEELING THAT
LOST,

JEANNIE SITTING BY THE FIRE,
NEEDS SOME BOY TO EARN
A DOLLAR,
ROLLED DOWN BESIDE HIM
ON THE FLOOR.
 JUST LIKE

NEED A WAY TO
BREAK THIS HEART
NEED A WAY TO STAND
THIS DOWN
ON A CORNER

TOUCH SENSITIVE
 NERVE AND BREAKING POINT
DAMAGE DONE,
 WITH NO REPAIR

STRETCHED THE LIMIT
SO FAR,
FELL TO PIECES AGAIN,
FEEL + COLD + WET MOIST,
AND STILL I'M DROWNING
AGAIN.

THERE'S A TIME + A PLACE,
WHEN FEELINGS
BLOCKED OUT AGAIN,
AND I ROLL TO ONE SIDE
I WAS DROWNING AGAIN.

A TASTE IN THE MOUTH
A NUMBING FEELING
RELIEF

IS RACING, SLOWING
RACING — STOPPED.
I REMEMBER NIGHTS
SPENT LISTENING TO
~~REMEMBER~~ UNTIL DAWN,
I REMEMBER NOTHING

DOOR SLOWLY OPENS,
JOHNNY SITS ON HIS
BOGO, LAYS DOWN
AND DIES

AND THERE'S A THOUSAND
REASONS LEFT TO WONDER
WHY, I JUST COULDN'T SEE,
HANGING ON TO NOTHING
CLUTCHING STRAWS, THAT
I COULDN'T SEE.
WALKING DOWN ANOTHER
ROAD THAT MEETS UP IN
THE END
TAKE A CARD, PICK
A CARD AND TAKE YOUR
CHOICE
solitary confinement

A RAMP TO THE TREES
AND TREES ALL AROUND.
I REMEMBER A TEAR,
FROZEN, WHITE ON
WHITE.
    I REMEMBER NOTHING

A GREY SALOON,
JOHNNY SIGHS,
WINDS DOWN THE WINDOW
AND STARES AT THE ROAD.

SOMETHINGS NEVER
MAKE SENSE. A FEAR
OF STEPPING OUT.
CROUCHED SHIVERING IN
THE CORNER, BLANKET
ROUND YOUR SHOULDER,
HOT THEN COLD, COLD
THEN WARM, PULSE

DOOR SLIDES OPEN,
JOHNNY CANCELS,
A VIEW FROM ABOVE.
~~HE~~ STICKS HIS HEAD
OUT OF THE WINDOW AND DRIES
HIS EYES.

~~TODAY~~

I REMEMBER A WINTER
SOME TIME AGO, ANGULAR
PATTERNS FORMED DEEP
IN THE GROUND WHERE
SOMEONE ONCE STOOD
WHITE ON BLACK,
WHITE ON WHITE.
ECHOED VOICES BOUNCING
OFF THE BUILDINGS AROUND,

KEEP ME FROM
INSIDE MY ~~HEAD~~

I REMEMBER NOTHING
CAN YOU HEAR
ME,
CAN'T YOU SEE

SET IN MOTION.

All the colours of
a shrunken world

480
9711/2

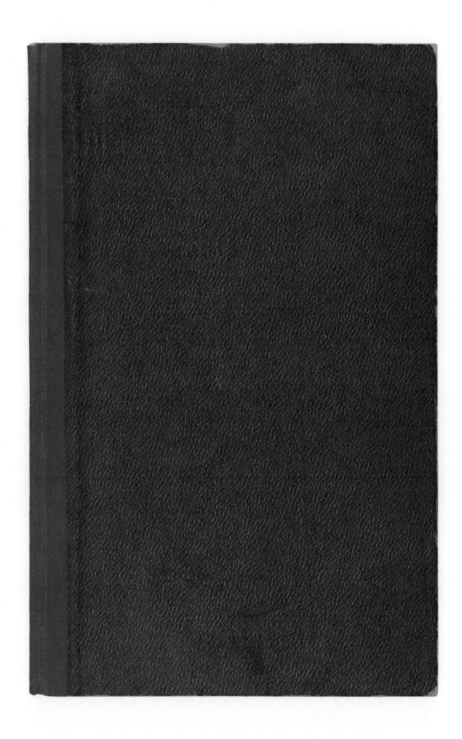

A LEGACY , SO FAR REMOVED
ONE DAY WILL BE IMPROVED,
ETERNAL RIGHTS . LEFT BEHIND,
WE WERE THE BETTER KIND,
TWO THE SAME, SET FREE TO.
I ALWAYS LOOKED TO YOU.

WE FOUGHT FOR GOOD, STOOD SIDE BY SIDE,
OUR FRIENDSHIP NEVER DIED,
ON STRANGER WAVES, THE LOWS + HIGHS
OUR VISION TOUCHED THE SKY,
CAPTIVE SOULS, TO PART TOO SOON
I PUT MY TRUST IN YOU.

A HOUSE SOMEWHERE ON FOREIGN SOIL,
WHERE AGEING LOVERS CALL,
I SAW YOUR GOAL, YOUR FINAL NEEDS,
WHERE DOGS + VULTURES EAT
SINK TO THIS , I TURNED TO GO
TO PUT MY TRUST IN YOU

EDGING TOWARDS , A CHILD
YOU MAY KEEP,
RETREADING THE BOARDS
PRETTY YOUNG THING
YOU'LL GET YOUR REWARD,
PERMISSION TO SPEAK
A PLACE TO YOURSELF
A GARDEN WITH SWINGS,
HANDWRITTEN CARDS
DONE NOTHING TO EASE,
THE BURDEN
WRITING IS MY RELEASE,
TO FACE UP TO THEM ALL,
AS THEY SWAY SIDE TO SIDE,
THEY PUT ME ON SHOWS,
DISGUSTS + REWINDS,
TO TAKE LIFE AWAY
WAS LIFE REALLY THERE,
NO SOUND, NO

YOU ALWAYS SAID YOU CARED,
UNTIL THE GUN WAS POINTED
OVER YOUR SOLDIER.
WENT WITH EVERYONE ELSE,
UNTIL YOU WERE IN A CORNER ALL
ALONE.

OH HOW I REALISED, HOW I
WANTED TIME.
PUT INTO PERSPECTIVE, TRY SO
HARD TO FIND.
JUST FOR ONE MOMENT, THOUGHT
I HAD MY WAY.
DESTINY UNFOLDED, WATCHED IT
SLIP AWAY.

I NEVER REALISED, THE LENGTHS I'D
HAVE TO GO,
ALL THE DARKEST CORNERS OF, A
SENSE I DIDN'T KNOW,
JUST FOR ONE MOMENT, I HEARD
SOMEBODY CALL, LOOKED BEYOND
THE DAY IN HAND, NO-ONE
THERE AT ALL.

THE AURA
PERCEPTION
ANTICIPATION
KINETIC OUTBURST
(OUT TAKE / INTAKE)
BORDERLINE
INSIDE THE LINE
AN ERROR OF JUDGEMENT
~~[scribbled out]~~
COLONY
THRESHOLD OF EXCESS
BALANCE OF POWER
LEVEL OF VIOLENCE
AURA OF
RETRIBUTION
CLEANSING OF THE SOUL
TWILIGHT OF THE IDOLS
SOMETHING MUST BREAK
CONFRONTATION
WHITE WALLS

LOST CONTROL
INTERZONE or ~~INTERZONE~~
~~[scribbled]~~ SHADOWPLAY
WILDERNESS
INSIGHT
CANDIDATE [REMEMBER NOTHING / DAY OF THE LORDS]
DISORDER ~~[scribbled]~~ / ~~[scribbled]~~
DIGITAL
GLASS
ATROCITY EXHIBITION

VOICE FROM THE WILDERNESS
UNKNOWN PLEASURES
SYMPTOMS OF COLLAPSE
~~[scribbled]~~
WILL OF THE UNDERWORLD
A CAUSE FOR ANXIETY
CONVULSING THERAPY
PASSOVER

1.  1 REMEMBER NOTHING.
2.  LEADERS OF MEN.
3.  WHEN THE NOISE STOPS.
4.  INDUSTRIAL WASTELAND
    - AN URBAN SOUNDTRACK

4.  TOUCH.
5.  AUTO - SUGGESTION.
6.  SOMEBODY ASKED ME THE WAY.
7.  I REMEMBER _____ NOTHING.


EXCESS

ON APPROVAL
UNKNOWN PLEASURES
EUROPEAN SON

BITTER AND TWISTED,
SEX AT THEIR FEET,
MOIST AND WELL SOFTENED
BY NIGHTS KEPT ON HEAT

PLEASE KEEP YOUR DISTANCE,
THE TRAIL LEADS TO HERE,
BLOOD ON YOUR FINGERS,
MARKED OUT OF FEAR.

4

COLLAPSED IN HIS BATHROOM,
SHE GAVE HIM HIS DUE,
BROKEN AND WOUNDED
HIS EYES LOOKED STRAIGHT THROUGH.

I CAMPAIGNED FOR NOTHING,
I WORKED HARD FOR THIS,
I TRIED TO ~~GE~~ GET TO YOU,
YOU TREAT ME LIKE THIS,

5

JUST SECOND NATURE,
ITS ALL THAT WE **KNOW**,
WE LIVE BY OUR OWN RULES,
AND ONLY DIRT SHOWS,

6

~~I LOOKED DOWN TO HIS FEET,~~
AND CALLED HIM BY NAME,
WHAT MAKES YOU SO DIFFERENT,
TO ME YOUR THE SAME.

I'VE GIVE IT EVERYTHING AND MORE,
I GAVE IT EVERYTHING I HAD,
~~[crossed out]~~
I ~~[crossed out]~~ IN THE ~~FACES~~ I KNEW,
IF ~~THAT~~ DON'T SUIT YOU, ~~ALL SO~~
~~BAD~~,
            WE NEED IT BAD.


WOKE UP IN ANOTHER FLESH,
DREAMED HE SAW ANOTHER
TIME,
TAKES IT FROM A DRAWER
AND SIGHS,
THIS COULD MAKE THEM
CHANGE THEIR MINDS,


MOVES TOWARD A CROWDED
SQUARE,
~~[crossed out]~~ CLEANS HIS HANDS
AND SHOUTS OUT LOUD,

# INTERZONE

SOMEONE TALKED ME IN TO <sup>TRY</sup> DO IT,
HAD TO CLOSE MY EYES TO GET
CLOSE TO IT,
SAW THE PLACE WHERE SHE'D A ROOM
TO STAY
SAW THE BED WHERE THE BODY LAY
AND I HAD NO TIME TO WASTE ~

HEARD A NOISE JUST A CAR OUTSIDE,
PULLED IN CLOSE BY THE BUILDINGS SIDE
HAD TO THINK COLLECT MY SENSES NOW,
FIND THE ~~ROOM~~ ~~ ~~ someone to FRIENDS DON'T
KNOW
I KNEW I HAD NO TIME TO WASTE

~~PAST THE FLOWERS ALL~~
~~ ~~ ~~ ~~ ~~ ~~ ~~NOW BY ROW,~~ I LOOKED ~~ ~~
~~ ~~ ~~ BEHIND~~ ~~ ~~ A WALL ~~ ~~ ~~ DOWN LOW
                                    A WARMER GLOW
INSERTED DEEP FELT ~~THE~~ ~~ ~~ GLOW,
NO TIME TO LOSE HAD TO KEEP
ON GOING
I GUESS ~ ~~DIED SOME TIME AGO~~

GETTING DARKER NOW,
FACES LOOK THE SAME,
~~KEPT~~ NO STOMACH, TORN APART
HAD TO THINK AGAIN,
TRYIN TO MOVE AWAY, HAD TO MOVE
AWAY + REACHED OUT.

WHITE WALLS, WHITE TILES, ~~LEGS~~
OF STEEL, TO MAKE YOU FEEL......
I REMEMBER NOTHING,

WHITE BOIS, NO NOISE, A FRESH
APPEAL, FROM WHERE WE STEAL—
I REMEMBER NOTHING.

DROWNING, YOU DROWNING,
YET THE WATERS SO WARM.
YOU LOOK ON IN,
I DID YOU NO HARM,

ONE MOMENT, UNTHINK,
THATS ALL THAT IT TOOK.
CONDEMNED NOW TO SILENCE,
YET SAFE FROM YOUR LOOK

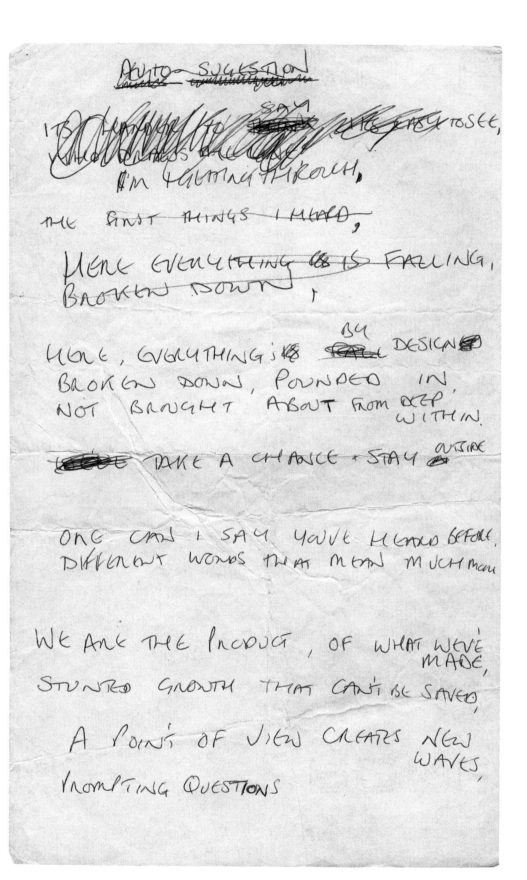

AUTO SUGGESTION

~~I ~~ SAY ~~EASY TO SEE,~~

I'M GETTING THROUGH,

THE FIRST THINGS I HEARD,

HERE EVERYTHING ~~IS~~ IS FALLING,
BROKEN DOWN,

BY
HERE, EVERYTHING IS ~~FELL~~ DESIGNED
BROKEN DOWN, POUNDED IN,
NOT BROUGHT ABOUT FROM DEEP
WITHIN.

~~~~ TAKE A CHANCE + STAY OUTSIDE

ONE CAN + SAY YOU'VE HEARD BEFORE,
DIFFERENT WORDS THAT MEAN MUCH MORE

WE ARE THE PRODUCT, OF WHAT WE'VE
MADE,
STUNTED GROWTH THAT CAN'T BE SAVED,

A POINT OF VIEW CREATES NEW
WAVES,
PROMPTING QUESTIONS

HOLLOW IN THEIR MEANING,
HOLLOW IN THEIR THINKING,
CAN'T YOU SEE ITS GETTING HARDER,
DEPRIVED OF ANY VISION,
LOCKED IN INDECISION,
DESTINATION GETTING FARTHER.

EUROPEAN BREAKDOWN,
NO PURPOSE IN THIS SHOWDOWN,
NO LOVE OF LIFE TO TAKE YOU HIGHER,
BURNING IN A NEW GUISE,
ALL YOU WANTS A NEW LIFE,

D.

HOLLOW IS THIS THINKING,
HOLLOW IS THE MEA[...]
CAN'T [...]

DRAWING CLOSE TO ~~ ~~ THOUSAND
WILKS ~~THAT~~ ~~BEGINNING~~ THE ~~NIGHT~~ LIGHT
UNKNOWING, UNDETECTED,

I STAND AROUND, WHILE PEOPLE GO,
I'M HANGING ON, JUST LET ME KNOW,

RESURRECTION, FOR THE GUILTY ONES,
DENUNCIATIONS, I'M THE ONLY ONE,
[ ROOM FULL OF PEOPLE, ROOM FOR JUST ONE
[ ROOM FOR THE MONEY, NO ROOM ~~ALSO~~ FOR
                                        NONE
MYSTERIES OF OLD, REVOLUTIONS, PEOPLE WERE
TOLD, AND TOMBS + SHRINES, RAIDS
COAST TO COAST, MALKET PLACE
BOUGHT + SOLD
COLD WERE HERE FINGERS, AS
ONWARD THEY RODE,
WE WERE IMMORTAL, WE WERE
ALL DEAD, WASHED UP ON THE
BEACHES, PROTECTED + FED,

CATHEDRAL SPIRES, I STAND ALONE,
ADMITTING TO NOTHING,

IF WE WERE IMMORTAL,
AND SO OUT OF REACH,
COMPARED WITH
WASHED UP ON THE BEACHES

PURE + FINE,          TWO WAYS TO CHOSE
A RAZORS EDGE,                LIKE FOR BOTH
                                          TOO SLOW
AND WENT STRAIGHT AHEAD,


TWO WAYS TO CHOSE,
ON A RAZONS EDGE,
    THOUGHT OUT ALOUD          REMAIN
                                                  BEHIND
    AND WENT STRAIGHT AHEAD,
ROOMFUL OF PEOPLE,     ROOM FOR
JUST ONE,    IF I CAN'T BREAK OUT
NOW,    THEN SURELY  I'm a

UBERMENSCHEN,

    TWO WAYS TO CHOSE,
    WHICH WAY TO GO,
    DECIDE FOR ME.
    PLEASE LET ME KNOW.

HAND ON MY SHOULDER, TELLS
        ME IM WRONG
    IF I COULD GET BACK TO,
        WHERE I BELONG

WHEN THE BEDROOMS SO COLD, ~~THEN~~

TO ~~DREAMS~~ OF ~~THE NIGHT~~ ALL THE
THOUGHTS CAN ESCAPE,

ALL NIGHTMARES SO OLD,

I'LL MAYBE FIND SOME FRIENDS
I CAN LEAD ASTRAY,

WITH NO APOLOGIES FOR ALL THESE
WORDS I SAY,

I'LL BURN THE OLD IDEALS + STAND FOR ALL
+ SCREAM FOR FUTURES SAKE TO SEE,

HOW DO YOU FEEL, WHEN IN THIS
COLONY

HOW CAN YOU THINK,

AND THE ROOMS ARE SO COLD,
NOW YOUR NOT HERE
NOW THAT

BUT THE PATHS
NOT SO CLEAR.

CRY OUT IN YOUR SLEEP ALL
MY FAILINGS EXPOSED,

TASTE IN MY MOUTH,

DESPERATION TAKES HOLD,

SOMETHING SO GOOD JUST CAN'T

WHEN *THOUGH* THERES STILL SOME APPEAL,
YET CAN'T EXPLAIN HOW YOU FEEL.
AND AMBITIONS RUN DRY.

YET YOUR BEDROOMS SO COLD, *THOUGH I CANT SAY JUST*
IS MY TIMING THAT FLAWED *WHY,*
*I CANT UNDERSTAND WHY*
TILL WE CANT FUNCTION NO MORE,
*HAS OUR     RUN DRY*

AND I WATCHED *AS*

TURN TO

TAKEN OUT
*THOUGH*
*NO ONE*
*CAN HEAR*
DID UN CRY OUT IN YOUR SLEEP, AS YOU'VE
*DONE ONCE* BEFORE.
ALL MY FAILINGS EXPOSED,
TAKE IT OUT IN YOUR DREAMS, *THOUGH THAT NO ONE*
AND I GAVE YOU

I CAN'T SEE ANYMORE,

WHY IS THERE STILL THIS APPEAL,
TO CAUSE

RESENTMENT,                    , MIXED
WITH LOVE + DESIRE,

TO IGNORE + TO
SAY FACE TO FACE THOUGH THERES
*NOTHING*
*TO SAY,*

FLAWED FAILINGS NEW DAY

wayward
submissive
ruthless

Cant function No more days
haze
ways

Is your bedroom so cold,
Personally flawed
MY TIMING

How can we sleep.
How can we eat.

TIRED BUT CAN'T SLEEP,
WHERE CAN WE GO,
HAS IT LOST ITS APPEAL,

HAVE YOU LOST MY APPEAL,
IN THESE REGRESSIVE DAYS,
CAN'T FUNCTION FOR LONG IN THIS
DEPRESSIVE HAZE.

Did you cry in your sleep,
ALL MY FAILINGS EXPOSED,
THERES THIS TASTE IN MY MOUTH,
TURNS ME

3 Take all kinds of
(all) for these days

I studied hard to stole
a way thru the modern
age

These days
- + says now

Looks straght a wde
all Joy
I've used all my time up
wayward
age

Stay for / re searched hard for you
and your
Sme special ways, in a
I used all my time
2
The mornings seem cold and

3 I'll drift along gladly if
be
you could stay
it

Nothing seems right now
feels
of place,
The mornings seem cold

I'd use lies and
Took all kinds
of insult, abuse
So pay our way,
Yet you can see
through me know
what I need
Will you stay
for these days
I'll use

I dirtied my hands
for pleasures sake

TOOK THREATS + ABUSE

~~ALL BEFORE SO WRONG NOW, PLANS~~
~~OUT OF~~ PLACE,
~~THE MORNINGS SEEM COLD ALMOST~~
~~OUT OF PLACE.~~

~~I STAND AND LOOK DOWN TILL~~
~~THE SILENCE BREAKS,~~
~~THESE MORNINGS SEEM STRANGE,~~
~~ALMOST OUT OF PLACE.~~

~~I SEARCHED HARD FOR YOU AND~~
~~YOUR SPECIAL WAYS,~~
~~I USED ALL YOUR TIME TILL I STILL~~
~~HOPED YOU'D STAY,~~

THESE MORNINGS SEEM STRANGE ALMOST
OUT OF PLACE,
I SEARCHED HARD FOR YOU AND YOUR SPECIAL
WAYS
THESE DAYS, THESE DAYS,
                        A KILLERS
I ~~USED~~ SPENT ALL YOUR TIME, ~~LEARNT~~ ^ ART

TOOK THREATS AND ABUSE TILL I'D LEARNT
THE PART
~~PLEASE~~ CAN YOU STAY, FOR THESE DAYS
              VISIONS OF BRIGHT ~~LINES~~ OUTWARD
                                        DECEPTION
ILL USE ~~KISS~~ ~~AND~~ ~~DISASTERS~~ TO GET
                                    ~~MY~~ MY WAY
                      OH OH
ILL USE HEARTBREAK ~~+~~ ROMANCE TO MAKE
                                    IT PAY.

IN THESE DAYS, THESE DAYS.

~~THERE~~ ~~ALL KINDS OF MADNESS~~
WELL DRIFT THRU IT ALL, THIS THE MODERN
                                    AGE.
~~TAKES~~ ~~NONE~~ OF IT ALL NOW ~~AS~~ THESE
                                    DAYS
                                    ARE DAYS

NEED TO IGNORE + TEAR UP
PREVIOUS INFLUENCES ¬— ~~BE~~
~~BE~~ LOOK AHEAD 'UNIMPORTANT.
" TASTE IS HABIT. THE REPETITION,
OF SOMETHING ALREADY ACCEPTED"
A TENDENCY TO MAKE SOMETHING 'WHY
~~~~ UNACCEPTABLE TASTEFUL TO
OTHER PEOPLE.

MANIPULATION — NO TIME FOR
SELF INDUCED - MANIPULATED BY
ANTI MANIPULATORS - SOCIALIST
GROUPS, WE etc

CONFUSION - OVERACTIVE, CULMINATION
OF IDEAS, FEELINGS,

POWER TO REASON — UNFORCED

ATROCITY EXHIBITION - USING
MISFORTUNE FOR GAIN.

THIS IS THE WAY ⟶
THIS IS THE WAY,
STRAIGHTEN YOUR TIE,
LOOK BESIDE YOU, LOOK ALL AROUND
+ STEP INSIDE.

WE TALK OF THE GOOD WE'VE DONE
~~THE~~ SOLUTIONS TO ALL ENDS
CAN'T YOU SEE WERE ALL PROSTITUTES,
WE COMMITT THE ATROCITIES,

~~████~~ ALL THIS CHARITY
CAN'T CHANGE DESTINY,
READ IT BUT CAN'T SEE 'IT,
WATCH IT CAN'T HEAR IT,
~~████~~ ALWAYS

YOU ~~████~~ SAID YOU CARED
UNTIL THE GUN WAS POINTED OVER
YOUR SHOULDER,
CRIED ALONG WITH EVERYONE ELSE
UNTIL YOU WERE IN A CORNER
AND ALONE,
~~████~~ THEY ARE THE CRIMINALS
WE ARE THEIR EXECUTIONERS.

Maybe
Just a stones throw from where your gonna
live,
An observer you say against your will,
Inbuilt reaction that says no all the time,
I look around . I cant see, well thats fine

Not just unfortunate victims of their fate
Or the horrors of some faraway place,
But every man, woman, children you ever see,
Who are burning on their own private schemes

OR IN FAITH BELIEVE you can SURVIVE,
RESTS ON THE WHIM OF
In asylums where the doors were opened wide,
And the rich paid to see Stepped Inside,
Convulsive movement
All holding mirrors

EXITS

AND POINTED OUT

WHIMS OF FANCY,

IN ARGENTS JUST FED TO STAY ALIVE
TO FIGHT FOR SPACE

Spectator

Just a stones throw from where your
gonna live.

now
past future

arenas

Not just unfortunate victims

man, mother
children

Or the horrors of a faraway
place

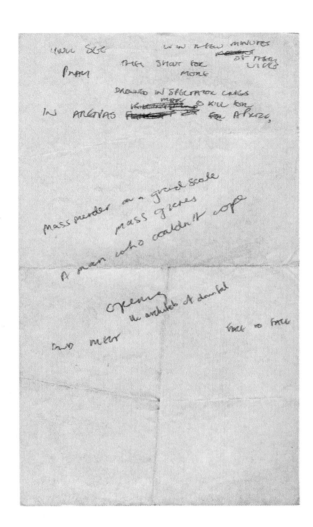
your SEE                    win a few minutes
                    THEY STAND FOR        OF MANY WARS
Proud                      MORE
                DROWNED IN SPECTATOR CASES
IN  ARGENTAS              MORE to KILL for
                                  for A PRIZE,

mass murder on a grand scale
mass graves
A man who couldn't cope

opening
the architect of doubtful

two meet                                FACE TO FACE

FEAR ~~NOT THAT~~ FINAL AWAKENING,
CRAWL ~~INTO YOUR DAYTIME CAGE~~,

FEAR OF THAT FINAL AWAKENING
THE QUAYSIDE IS SO COLD AT NIGHT,
A WAREHOUSE SO OLD YET STILL
                                    STANDING
A COIN IN THE WATER FOR LUCK.

Fear of that final awakening

ON WHICH· I NEED to
                          SURVIVE.

A WAYWARD

              ER
A ~~NEW~~ BRIGHTNESS        AND WAYWARD DISTRACTION

MARK JAMES
CHRIS BROOKS

PALE WHITE LIGHT TO THE KITCHEN FLOOR,
INSECT FLIGHT MOTHER NATURES LAW,
A NORMAL AGE ~~WHEN LIFE BEGAN~~
            DRUNKEN INSINCERE,
    THIS IS THE MOMENT I WANTED SO MUCH

THIS IS MY CRISIS.
THROUGH FAULTS OF MY OWN,
DRIVING ME UNDER, AWAY FROM THE
NOTIONS ~~THING~~ KEPT SINCE A CHILD.

THIS IS MY HEARTACHE
A WEB OF DESIRE
PURGING THE FRESHNESS, TAINTING
I

THIS IS MY DISTURBANCE,
THROUGH MOMENTS OF _____

DESTROYING THE ORDER + INBUILT
PROTECTION IVE KEPT SINCE A CHILD

            KNOWING ID LOSE A
                                TIME

RESPONSIBILITIES BACKED OUT OF

I WITNESSED THE DEATH OF A 1000
    YOUNG MEN, BUT COULDN'T DO
    NOTHING     AT ALL

IS THIS IS THE ROLE THAT YOU WANTED
SO ~~much~~, MUCH
HANDED TO YOU ON A PLATE,
EXPLICITLY MOULDED, FORCED INTO SHAPE
IT ALL FALLS APART ON FIRST TOUCH,
AND THIS IS YOUR CRISIS
A FRIEND ~~~~ STOPPED TO ASK,

a ~~personal touch~~ BRUTALITY        BRUTAL DISRUPTION,

                                        CONTAINED
THIS IS my ~~~~ CRISIS CONFINED ~~to~~ A FEW
          OR WAIT FOR THE TIME IT WILL


THIS IS THE ~~~~ CRISIS, I KNEW HAD TO
                                    COME,
~~~~
DESTROYING THE BALANCE ID KEPT,
PURGING THE ~~~~ AND THEN
TURNING AWAY,
~~YOU~~ ~~~~ ~~~~ ~~~~ ~~ON FIRST~~
~~~~.

THOSE WHO ~~~~ REACHED ~~~~ INTO
THE DEPTHS,

    ~~NEXT~~              UNFOLD IN AN HOUR


~~CAN THIS BE WHAT WILL COME NEXT~~

THIS IS THE CRISIS I KNEW HAD TO COME, ~~too much~~
DESTROYING THE BALANCE ID KEPT,
THINKING ABOUT ~~~~ WHAT MIGHT HAVE BEEN,
AND WONDERING WHAT WILL COME NEXT

THIS IS THE CRISIS I KNEW HAD COME,
DESTROYING THE BALANCE I'D KEPT,
TURNING AROUND TO THE NEXT SET OF LIVES,
WONDERING WHAT WILL COME NEXT,
IS THIS THE ROLE THAT YOU WANTED TO LIVE
I WAS FOOLISH TO ASK FOR TOO MUCH,
H ~~I TOOK~~ ~~FROM~~ YOU,
WITHOUT THE PROTECTION, REMOTE~~NESS~~ +.
IT ALL FALLS APART AT FIRST TOUCH.

~~THIS IS THE DISTURBANCE~~, A MOTION AWAY,
~~HANDED TO~~ ~~ON A PLATE,~~
WATCHING IT ~~DRAIN~~.

very good
its A
pathetic
(at the
same
time not)

WATCHING THE DAY AS IT COMES TO
CLOSE,
BRUTALLY TALKING ITS TIME
PEOPLE ARE TRADED FOR (WEAPONS + GUNS) POLITICAL, MEANS
ITS HAPPENING ALL OF THE TIME, OF EVENTS
CAN I GO ON WITH THIS ~~ORDER~~ OF TRAINS
~~THINGS,~~
DISTORB~~ANCE~~ ING + PURGING MY ~~MIND,~~ LIFE
OR BACK OUT OF ~~RESPON~~ MY DUTIES
WHEN ALLS SAID AND DONE,
I KNOW THAT ~~I'LL~~ the LOSE EVERY TIME.

MOVING ALONG IN OUR OWN ~~SEPAR~~
WAYS,
CUTTING OUR THROATS BY THE FIRE
SWIMMING AGAINST ALL WE WANTED TO
DO
DROWNING AGAIN EVERY HOUR,
IS THIS THE GIFT THAT I WANTED.
TO GIVE,
~~KEEPIN AWAY OUT OF SIGHT~~
PROBLEMS + NONE OF THEM SOLVED,
IM LOOKING AT YOU FOR THE VERY FIRST TIME,

THIS IS THE HOUR WHEN THE
~~MANIACS~~ RETURNS
~~Is~~ STRANGERS went ~~too~~ ALWAYS LATE ~~Not to~~
~~LEAD~~

A MOMENT SO MOVING GOES
STRAIGHT TO YOUR HEART,
~~AND THEN CUTS ACROSS AS YOU~~
WAIT BUT GRADUALLY CHANGES TO HATE.

A Pattern is set a reaction
will start,
complete but rejected too soon,
Thinking ahead in the grip of
each ~~fear~~,
But Nothing will keep me from you.

Pursuing that moment when all
will be right,
A ~~fault~~ that's been buried
for years,
The pitfalls so great, its so
hard to ~~connect~~ reflect
The attraction that brought me
to ~~here~~, Through Jungles of deadwood + other
~~use it~~ places I never could get

This is the hour when the young
men return
    Strangers in ~~time too late~~ oh where have ~~they~~
    ~~gardens of theres~~ ~~forget been~~
A moment so moving, goes straight
to your heart,
And then ~~gets~~ right into your skin,
A Pattern is set a reaction will
start,
A Montage of every thought,
Compiled and rejected its all
~~beside Wall~~
    But nothing will keep ~~us apart~~
                                me
    away

~~And~~ your shadows that ~~danced~~ moved in
the light at ~~each~~ ~~your~~ day
How could I ever forget,

3 A    moment   thats   so moving it hits
    at your heart
4 But doesn't get into your
    A Pattern is set, a reaction will
                                    start
    Against


    How could I ever forget.

    Nothing could keep us apart.

1 This   is the   time   when the
    —   reaccurs,   1o this be time when
                      appear
1

    Walk with me
    Take Hold + See.
                        are making it
    + people   I d only give met hand

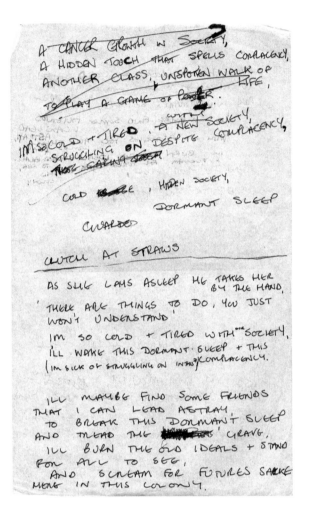

A CANCER GROWTH IN SOCIETY,
A HIDDEN TOUCH THAT SPELLS COMPLACENCY,
ANOTHER CLASS, UNSPOKEN WALK OF
TO PLAY A GAME OF POWER.      LIFE,

IM SO COLD + TIRED   WITH A NEW SOCIETY,
STRUGGLING ON  DESPITE COMPLACENCY,
THOSE SAVING SOUL

      COLD     , HIDDEN SOCIETY,
                DORMANT SLEEP

      GUARDED

## CLUTCH AT STRAWS

AS SHE LAYS ASLEEP HE TAKES HER
                         BY THE HAND,
'THERE ARE THINGS TO DO, YOU JUST
WON'T UNDERSTAND'
IM SO COLD + TIRED WITH SOCIETY,
ILL WAKE THIS DORMANT SLEEP + THIS
(IM SICK OF STRUGGLING ON IN THIS COMPLACENCY.

ILL MAYBE FIND SOME FRIENDS
THAT I CAN LEAD ASTRAY,
   TO BREAK THIS DORMANT SLEEP
AND  TREAD THE         GRAVE,
   ILL BURN THE OLD IDEALS + STAND
FOR ALL TO SEE,
   AND  SCREAM FOR FUTURES SAKE
HERE IN THIS COLONY.

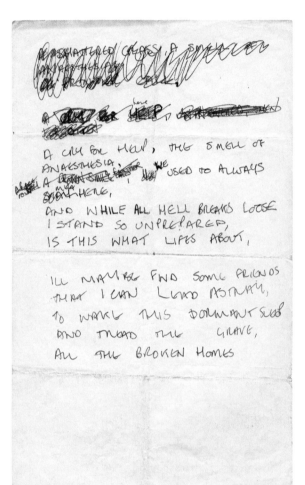

A CRY FOR HELP, THE SMELL OF
ANAESTHESIA,
A             , WE USED TO ALWAYS
SAY HERE,
AND WHILE ALL HELL BREAKS LOOSE
I STAND SO UNPREPARED,
IS THIS WHAT LIFES ABOUT,

ILL MAYBE FIND SOME FRIENDS
THAT I CAN LEAD ASTRAY,
TO WAKE THIS DORMANT SLEEP
AND TREAD THE     GRAVE,
ALL THE BROKEN HOMES

COLONY

A CRY FOR HELP, A HINT OF ANAESTHESIA,
THE SOUND FROM BROKEN HOMES WE USED
TO ALWAYS MEET HERE,
A PARENTS WORRIED GLANCE, A LOOK
THAT REASSURES, (TELLS THE STORY)
HE DIDN'T STAND A CHANCE, COULDN'T
EVEN SPEAK THE WORDS. (HOW COULD
THEY DO THIS
TO ME)

CAN YOU HELP ME, CAN YOU
SPARE SOME TIME,

AS SHE LAYS ASLEEP, HE TAKES
HER IN HIS ARMS, IN HIS HAND
THERE ARE THINGS TO DO
AND I DON'T WISH YOU HARM
(YOU'LL NEVER UNDERSTAND,)

A NEWSREEL CLIP, A CUE FOR CONFRONTATION
ANTAGONISTIC CAUSING DISLOCATION,
A LIGHT OF BLUE SWATCH
HIM GO ASTRAY,
UNFRIENDLY VOICE JUST SAYS HES GONE
AWAY.

APOLOGISES WHEN HER THOUGHTS ARE SHOWN
WHERE HER BOYS HAVE GONE GOD
ONLY KNOWS,
THE WORDS SHE READS JUST MAKE HER FEEL
UNEASY,
AS SHE REMEMBERS LIGHTING OF
THE COLONY.

WHO GIVES THE RIGHT, + NOW IT MUST BE
BROKEN,
DRAGGED RIGHT OUT, + PLACED IN THE OPEN,
WHILE THE IN THEMS SEEM TO ALL RUN FREE,
BUT WHO ARE THOSE IN THIS COLONY.

kept apart

ETERNAL RIGHTS, SO FAR REMOVED
ONE DAY WILL BE IMPROVED,
You CONSCIENCE MOVED, TO TOUCH THE
                                    BLIND
WE WERE THE BETTER KIND.

AS WE WOKE UP THIS EVENING,
I THOUGHT ABOUT MY MIND
                        FUNCTION,
IS THIS FUNCTIONAL AT ALL,
THRU THE TREMBLING OF MY
                        FINGERS
I COULD SEE ALL SENSES FALL,

WHAT I'M FEELING SHOULD
BE THE LAST
THE LAST PAGE,
LIKE EVERY PAGE SHOULD
BE THE LAST.

A SHALLOW GAME, SO FAR REMOVED,
ONE DAY WILL BE IMPROVED,
TORMENTS YET CALMS, THOUGH STILL I FIND
WE WERE THE SWEETEST KIND,
I'LL ALWAYS CARE, WE ALWAYS KNEW
I ALWAYS LOOKED TO YOU.

THEIR PREJUDICE, THAT POINTS TO ME,
STRANGER - STILL INCOMPLETE,
SEE HOW THEY LAUGH, HOW THEY KNOW
THEIR KIND JUST COME + GO,
IMMORTALISTS, BUT WHERE WERE YOU,
I PUT MY TRUST IN
I ALWAYS LOOKED TO YOU.

A TOWN SOMEWHERE, ON FOREIGN SOIL,
WHERE AGENCY LOVERS CALL,
IS THIS YOUR CARE, SUPPLIES YOUR
NEEDS,
WHERE DOGS + VULTURES FEED, EAT,
COMMITTED STILL I HAD TO GO
I PUT MY TRUST IN YOU.


A PROMISED LEGACY THAT FOLLOWED ME
THROUGH ALL THE YEARS AND ON,
I PUT MY TRUST IN YOU,
AND THOUGH THE DOORS ARE CLOSED
I'LL ALWAYS CARE FOR THOSE
WHO COULDN'T CARRY ON,
THEY PUT THEIR TRUST IN YOU,
ACCEPTED AND DISMISSED TOO,
THE WAY EVERYTHING GOES,

WRITTEN THERE FOR ALL, STEPPED
ON FOREIGN SOIL, UNEASY
TASK TO MEET,
I ALWAYS LOOKED TO YOU,

ALWAYS CARE

A SHALLOW GAME, FOR FOOLS TO PLAY,
IMMORTAL

COMMITTED TO HIS
where agency lovers call

CAN COME + GO

# HEART AND SOUL

INSTINCTS THAT CAN STILL BETRAY
US.
A JOURNEY THAT LEADS TO THE SUN,
SOULLESS ~~THAT~~ AND BENT ON ~~LEADS TO~~ DESTRUCTION
A STRUGGLE BETWEEN RIGHT +
WRONG.

YOU TAKE MY PLACE IN THE
SHOWDOWN
I'LL OBSERVE WITH A PITIFUL EYE,
AND HUMBLY ASK FOR FORGIVENESS,
A ~~BASIC~~ REQUEST WELL BEYOND
YOU AND I.

AN ABYSS THAT LAUGHS AT CREATION,
A CIRCUS COMPLETE WITH ALL FOOLS,
~~A STONE~~
~~OR~~ FOUNDATIONS THAT LASTED THE AGES,
AND THEN
~~HEARTS~~ ~~TORN~~ RIPPED APART AT ~~THEIR~~ ITS
THEIR
ROOTS.

BEYOND ALL THIS GOOD IS THE
TERROR,
THE GRIP OF A MERCENARY~~S~~ HAND,
WHEN SAVAGERY TURNS ALL GOOD
                        REASON,
THERE'S NO TURNING BACK — NO LAST
    STAND

EXISTENCE WELL WHAT DOES IT
MATTER,
  I EXIST ON THE BEST TERMS
I CAN,
 THE PAST IS NOW PART OF MY
FUTURE,
    THE PRESENT IS ~~WELL~~ OUT
OF HAND.

PROCESSION MOVES ON, THE SCREAMING ~~SHOUTING~~
IS OVER,
~~JUST WHATS GOING ON~~, ~~NO-ONE WILL~~
~~FEEL~~, (RAISING THE GLORY OF ~~THOSE~~ NOW GONE) LOVED ONES
TALKING ALOUD AS THEY SIT ROUND
THEIR TABLES,
SCATTERING FLOWERS, WASHED
DOWN BY THE RAIN.

PLAYED BY THE GATE AT THE ~~FENCE~~ OF FOOT
THE GARDEN,
WATCHING THEM PASS LIKE CLOUDS
IN THE SKY,
TRY TO CRY OUT IN THE HEAT OF
THE MOMENT,
[ IF ONLY THEY KNEW I HAD SOMETHING ]
TO SAY.

CRY LIKE A CHILD THOUGH ~~MY~~ THESE YEARS
~~AND~~ ~~GROW OLDER~~ MAKE ME
WITH CHILDREN MY TIME IS SO WASTEFULLY
SPENT,
A BURDEN TO KEEP, ~~BY~~ THEIR INNER THOUGH
COMMUNIONS
[ ~~BUT MY~~ REFLECTION ~~ARE SO CLEAR, I SEE~~ ]
~~THROUGH~~ ~~FALSE GRIEF~~, AN UNLUCKY DEAL
ACCEPT LIKE A CURSE.
STOOD BY THIS GATE AT THE FOOT OF
THE GARDEN,
MY WORLD STRETCHES OUT FROM THE
FENCE TO THE WALL,
CONTINOUS PROCESS, ALL IMAGE
UNBROKEN,
WHERE FANTASY ENDS, I DON'T
KNOW AT ALL

GOT RID OF THIS HEADACHE, I THINK
ITS THE WEATHER,
THE CLIMATE IS RIGHT TO ADJUST
TO THEIR NEEDS,
LOOK THROUGH THE EYES OF AN
IMBECILES NOTIONS,
ALL SHOWS SO CLEAR, CONFUSION
+ ALL,

PLAYED BY THE GATE AT THE
FOOT OF THE GARDEN,
WATCHING THEM PASS LIKE
CLOUDS IN THE SKY,
THE PURPOSE SEEMS CLEAR IN
THE COLD OF THE MORNING,
THERE'S MORE GOING ON
THAN FIRST MEETS THE EYE,

ACCEPT LIKE A CURSE, AN UNLUCKY
DEAL

AN IDIOTS WORDS WON'T CARRY
MUCH WEIGHT

The morning is cold but seems fine fo me
POSSESSED by

BACKING AWAY

MY AGE STANDING STILL
NEVER TO CHANGE
YOU'VE BEEN IN MY PLACE THOUGH
YOU WON'T CARE TO MENTION,
YOUR CONCERN DOESN'T COUNT
FOR YOUR FORGOTTEN YET,

STOOD BY THE GATE AT THE FOOT OF THE
GARDEN,
WATCHING THEM PASS LIKE CLOUDS IN THE
SKY,
INCIDENTS HANG IN THE AIR FOR A
MOMENT,
THEN BACK TO — — AND DRIFT QUIETLY
BY.

KOMAKINO

~~WE SEEMED~~ ALWAYS SO FARAWAY.
NO CHANCE TO STRAIGHTEN OUT,
~~THEY~~ ~~littns~~ HERE TO ~~PAY~~ STAY
LINE THE ROADS EN ROUTE,
HEAVEN MADE CASTAWAY
THAT BRINGS ME BACK TO YOU.

ONE MOMENT MOVES ~~YOU~~ US SO
IT GOES STRAIGHT TO OUR
HEARTS,
BUT WHEN COURAGE STARTS
TO GO,
PERSISTENCE CAN'T GO FAR,
A ~~DEARLY~~ COMPLIMENT
NO NICER,

~~CAN ONLY DO YOU HARM~~

AVENUES ALL LINED WITH TREES,
EDENS GARDEN LEFT FOR THIEVES,
I LOOKED UPON AN EMPTY STAGE,
WHERE ALL THE YOUNG MEN ONCE HAD
                              PLAYED.

INROADS LEADING ON AND ON,
FILLED WITH STRANGERS EVERY ONE,
THE        ARRIVED AND HERE TO STAY,
LOOK THEN TURN THEIR HEADS AWAY.

BUILDINGS TORN DOWN TO THE GROUND,
REPLACED BY NEW ONES THAT~~~~ MORE
                            SOUND,

AND AS TORCHES GLOW RIGHT
THRU THE NIGHT,         ALL THATS
A SACRIFICE FOR ~~~~~~~ LIGHTS.

I LOOKED AHEAD AN EMPTY SPACE,
A LIFETIMES ~~~~~~~ ERASED,


AVENUES ALL LINED WITH TREES
AND YOUNG MEN ~~WALKING,
HOW COULD THEY ) TAKE IT AWAY
AND LEAVE,
(          IT LOOKING THIS WAY,


AVENUES ALL LINED WITH TREES AND
YOUNG MEN | WALKING, ~~~~~~~~~~
HOW COULD THEY-
TAKE IT AWAY
AND LEAVE IT.
LOOKING THIS WAY.
                        AND INROADS
MOUNTAIN TRAILS ~~~~ ~~~~ TO
FAMILIES ALL ALONG,
WHY DID THEY,
TAKE MY HOME AWAY,
WHAT USE IS IT
ANYWAY.

EDENS GARDEN LEFT IN RUINS
WE WERE SCARRED FOR LIFE,
A LAST ACT | OF BETRAYAL
AND NOW
      WE ALL ARE BLAME

ceased ~~[scribbled out text]~~

DAYS, MONTHS HAVE SLIPPED BY,
TRIED TO PAY IT ALL BACK,
BEEN WAITING TILL THE TIDE TURNED,
ON BEACHES WHERE THE PAST BURNED
AWAY JUST LONG,

PLAYED A WAITING GAME,
OPPORTUNITIES TAKEN, SLIPPED BACK IN AGAIN,
TEMPORARY MEASURE TILL THE URGE
                                    CAME,

BUT THE LIFEBLOOD HAD DRAINED,
COMPULSION HAD CEASED,

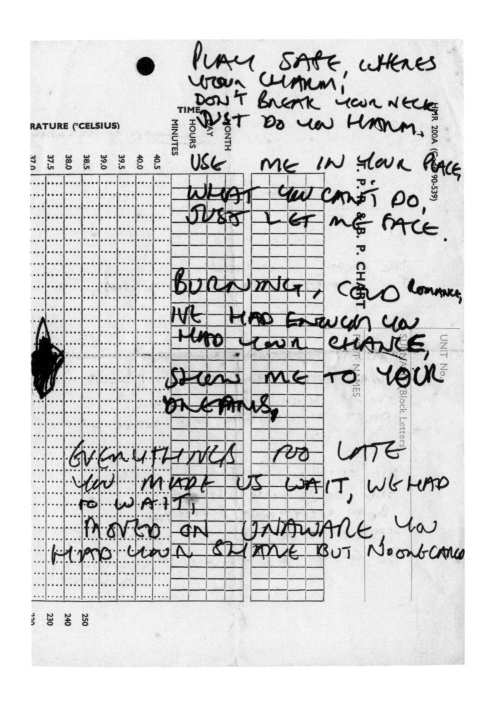

SURE ILL SEE YOU DOWN,
YOU DO FOR ME . I DID FOR YOU.
THOUGHTS JUST BRING ME DOWN.
THE DOWN FOR GOOD
THATS UNDERSTOOD.

GUESS WERE THINKIN NOW.
SHOULD WE TAKE SIDES, ~~YOUR ~~ OR STAY OUTSIDE
BUT THINGS JUST STAY THE SAME,
THE SHIT REMAINS . WITH DIFFERENT NAMES.

IVE BEEN ~~MOVING~~ MOVING ,
TO MAYBE THE NEXT PHASE,
NO SITTING ON THE FENCE.
ALL OPTIONS NEVER SAFE.

IVE BEEN SEARCHING,
FOR SOMETHIN MORE THAN THIS,

4.

FALLOUT FROM INSIDE
YOUVE LOST YOUR TOUCH , IT DRIVES ME WILD
THINK YOUR IN THE CHAIR,
DONT THINK FOR ME, WELL WAIT +
SEE.

NO TIME LEFT TO TAKE,
ILL GIVE MY SHARE,
BUT NO THINGS THERE,
TAKE YOU DOWN WITH ME,
SO GET THE TASTE, (YOUVE USED
TO WASTE.)

MEMORANDUM

To:

From:

Ref:

Date:

_____

AN EXPEDITION DOOMED TO FAIL,
WHAT NEW CONQUESTS SHALL WE
SEEK,
TO REACH OUT A HELPING HAND,
THE WEARY + THE WEAK
THE HELPLESS + THE BLIND,
AS I STAND AND LOOK HEAD,
AS THE MERCENARIES TAKE STANDS,

ON HALLOWED GROUND,
THE MAN WHO WOULD FINALLY
ESCAPE FROM ALL SENSE OF
BELONGING AND PERMANENCE,
CLUTCHING AT STRAWS,
GRASPING A HAND THAT
BREAKS THROUGH ALL BARRIERS
OF SELF RESPECT AND OUTWARD
SELF CONTROL

WHAT ARE YOUR VALUES?

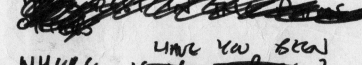

WHERE ~~IS TOO THAT~~ HAVE YOU BEEN ?

WHERE ARE GOING.

ON IMPULSE WITHOUT NO REGRET,
WITH GIFTS OF THAT YOU HANG ROUND
YOUR NECK
ON JOURNEYS THAT END WHERE THEY
START,
BY PRE-MEDITATED ATTACKS.


PEOPLE JUST STAND

DOWN CARE

TO PLACES WE DON'T WANT GO,
OBJECTIONS THAT FROZE & ~~WON'T~~
SHOW,                        CAN'T
ON JOURNEYS THAT END WHERE  THEY
START.
JUST HANGING AROUND FOR SOME
PART

THIS IS THE WAY WE SPEND TIME.

ON UNWANTED GIFTS ~~FOR OUR~~
~~FRIENDS, HID~~ HID AWAY
TO HANG ROUND THEIR NECKS
FOR ONE DAY,

WAS GAINED

NOT YOUR WORLD
NOT IN MY TIME

THE HONOURS, THE TRAPPINGS,
DISGUST FOR SUBNORMAL, DOES
THIS MAKE A MAN, MAKES
MISTAKES ALL THE TIME, BUT
DON'T HURRY TO GET THERE,
YOU'LL TRIP OVER MURDERS
YOU MADE FOR YOURSELF, TO
CATCH OUT THE UNTHINKING
WHO CANT THINK FOR
BARRIERS PUT THERE TO HELP
YOU EXIST.

IS THIS YOUR WORLD

SOMEONE CALLED HER NAME!!
CHILDLIKE SENSES SAFES AT HOME
.RIGHT
now,

SOMEONE CALLS HER NAME,
A NOISE OUTSIDE. ~~DENT~~ BREAKS
THE SILENCE SOMEHOW.

AREN'T YOU GLAD I CAME?
I NEED SOMEONE TO REALISE MY
DREAMS,
NAME
I ~~WALKED HERE~~ ALL THIS WAY,
I HEARD IT SAID THIS PLACE
IS RIGHT FOR TWO.


SOMEONE CALLS HER NAME,
ALL DIVERSIONS LOOKS THE
SAME WAY,
NO TIME TO THINK OF CHANGE,

NO ONE KNOWS , NO ONE CARES ANYHOW

WHATS YOUR REASONS , WHATS YOUR THINKING,

SURE IVE SEEN

MOVING FROM LEFT + TO RIGHT
MIXED UP IN IT ALL,
WHAT ARE YOUR REASONS,
WRAPPED UP IN HELL

THE YEAR ZERO

TAKE A LOOK IN TO ~~THE~~ TWILIGHT ZONE,
THEY PICKED A YEAR IN WHICH TO
~~START IT~~ FROM,
LANDSCAPE TROUBLED BY A VIOLENT
STORM,
THAT RIPPED THE HEART OUT +

HE CAN'T UNDERSTAND WHY IT
SHOULD BE THIS WAY,
HE CAN'T UNDERSTAND WHAT MAKES
THEM THINK THIS WAY,
HE WANDERED IN ONE DAY

CURSE THE POWERS

ANTI CHRIST LEGACY
EXPERIMENTING WISELY

DONT THINK I~~D~~ LEAVE STAYED ^JUST^ FOR ONE
MORE DAY.
IT~~B~~ SEEMS SO MUCH LIKE HOME
NO~~W~~ ^ROOM^ TO GO ASTRAY,
DONT THINK I COULD WATCH - WITH
MINDLESS ,EMPTY ~~EYES~~ ~~~~, ~~IT'S~~ STASIS
INTAKE MOVING IN , FORCED TO WALK
A LONELY PATH,

PICTURES ALL AROUND, OF HOW GOOD
A LIFE SHOULD BE,
A MODEL FOR THE REST , THAT BRED
~~INFERIORITY~~ INSECURITY,
I WALKED A JAGGED LINE + THEN
CAME BACK FOR MORE,
ITS ALWAYS IN MY MIND, AN
INSTITUTION WITH NO ~~GOD'S~~ LAW,

IN THE BACK OF MY MIND,
ALL I FEEL IS MISTRUST,
IN THE BACK OF MY MIND
ALL I SEE IS THE DIRT,
SEGREGATION OF THOUGHTS,
IDEALS TURNING TO DUST


WHERE SOME HOUSES ONCE
STOOD,
STANDS A MAN WITH A GUN,
IN SOME ~~XXXX~~ NEIGHBORHOOD,
A FATHER HANGS HIS SON,
IN THE BACK OF MY MIND,

WHERE YOU GOING TO RUN TO NOW
WHERE YOU GONNA HIDE,
ALL THE DREAMS YOU EVER HAD IN TATTERS AT YOUR SIDE,
THINKING ON YOUR OWN OF EVERY SMALL MISTAKE.
NEVER TOOK THE CHANCE WITH EVERYTHING AT STAKE

TO TAKE THE BLAME

STARING IN THE MIRROR AT EVERYTHING YOU'VE SEEN

LOOK INTO THE FUTURE NOW
+ SEE WHAT MIGHT HAVE BEEN

IN THE BACK OF MY MIND
GOT A TICKET TO US.

WHERE SOME HOUSES ONCE STOOD,
STANDS A MAN WITH A GUN,

BRIDGES WON'T HOLD
TOMORRO WITH LININGS OF GOLD,
AND THE CELLARS ARE COLD

HE TRIED FOR EVERYTHING + MORE,
UNSETTLED MOMENTS , WANTED MORE,
ENDURED DIVERSIONS , FELT LIKE
                                  MORE,
STOPPED THE CAR + CRIED FOR
                                  MORE.


I HELD ON ON BUT IT ALL GOT
                         TOO MUCH,
THAT SOMETHING ~~ELSE~~ THAT I
                      COULDN'T
                       TOUCH.

   I KNEW THEN THAT WE'D MADE
A MISTAKE,
   WE TURNED OUR HEADS HOPING
SOMETHING WOULD BREAK
                      IS REAL

ARE...WE THE SHALLOW KIND,
JUSTIFIED TO SPEAK OUR MINDS,
FOR BETTER OR WORSE, IN SICKNESS
                              + MORE
PICTURE THIS IN YOUR LEFT- BEHIND

I'LL WORK THE FIELDS AND JUST WATCH
                              YOU PLAY
BORN IN THE HEAT LET YOU TALK ALL
                              DAY.
~~WELLS~~ / ~~GAME~~
A FOOLS GAME MAY YOUR EYES RUN
                              RED,
A ~~FOOL~~ TO THINK

~~PLAYING A GAME~~

BURNING HEAT ~~FOR AFQUIET PLACE~~ LIKE AN ACT OF GOD,
A FOOLISH GAME   AGAINST ALL ODDS,

<u>OVERCROWDING</u>

FACES PRESSED FLAT AGAINST GLASS
TEN MEN IN A ROOM FOR TWO, WINDOWS,
CENSORSHIP STOPS HERE,
NO ISOLATION,
ONLY DE TOXIFICATION,

ABNORMAL RELATIONSHIPS FORMED,
IN CORNERS AND ON FLOORS,
BREATHLESS, BREEDING AND CRAMPED
ON ALL FOURS
NO VIEW, NO SENSE OF TIME.

IT WAS A STRANGE WAY TO GO

AND BODIES ALL AROUND
PUSHING TO HEAR
PLEASE LET ME IN.

BUILDINGS ~~STRUCTURE~~ PROJECTS ~~THEIR~~ ~~OPEN~~
~~BROKEN~~
~~WALLS~~ ~~PUSHING TO~~ ~~FORWARD~~, STATION

THE THIEVES LIE IN WAIT, TRAPPED
IN THEIR SNARE

ALWAYS IN VIEW, BUT I NEVER
STARE,
    KNOCKING DOWN WALLS,
    DON'T LET ME IN,

THREATENED BY LIFE ITSELF,
THREATENED BY YOU
            BY ME

POLITICAL — PARTY POLITICS — SOCIOLOGICAL SENSE
SUGGESTS A CERTAIN SET OF IDEALS + BELIEFS ADOPTED
OR ADOPTED FOR — SOCIOLOGICAL GOVERNING
EVERYDAY LIVING PRICES, LAWS, MOTIVES
CALCULATED.

MORE IN EMOTIONAL SENSE — REALITY
RATHER THAN IDEALISTIC IE SOCIOLOGICAL. IMPULSIVE
IRRATIONAL, MOTIVES UN PREMEDITATED
UNORGANISED —

CORRUPTION — MUSIC BIZ, GOVERNMENT.
BUSINESS — EVERYTHING. DUAL STANDARDS
HYPOCRISY. RESTRICTIONS

THOSE WITH NO CHOICE — SOCIAL
OR INTELLECTUAL POSITION HOLDS NO
BRIGHT PROSPECTS FOR FUTURE. TRAPPED
IN CORNERS. — SOLITARY.

EXPERIMENTATION — MUSIC, FILMS,
RADIO STATIONS — MORE CONTROL
UNLIKELY TO HAPPEN IN NEAR
FUTURE GOING BY TODAYS POLITICAL
+ ECONOMIC CLIMATE.

NO NEW EMERGENT FORCES OR
POLICIES LIKELY TO CHANGE.
MORE RETURN TO DARK AGES
DISSIDENTS

SLEEP THROUGH THIS DARKNESS,
IN PLACE AS YOU ~~GO~~ I GO
SHOCKED BY MY PRESENCE,
STRIKE ONE FINAL BLOW.

# APPENDIX TWO

## ARTWORK, FANZINES, BOOKS, LETTERS

A FRACTURED MUSIC · A FACTORY RECORD · ALL RIGHTS OF THE MANUFACTURER AND OF THE OWNER OF THE RECORDED WORK RESERVED

*f*

| 27·6·80 | FAC 23-12B | | 45 | STEREO |

Joy Division
**These Days**
**Love Will Tear Us Apart**

Produced by Martin Hannett
Published by Fractured Music

A FRACTURED MUSIC · A FACTORY RECORD · ALL RIGHTS OF THE MANUFACTURER AND OF THE OWNER OF THE RECORDED WORK RESERVED

*f*

| 9/5/80 | FACT. 25 | | STEREO | 33 |

Joy Division

"Closer"

Produced by Martin Hannett
Published by Fractured Music

APPENDIX TWO

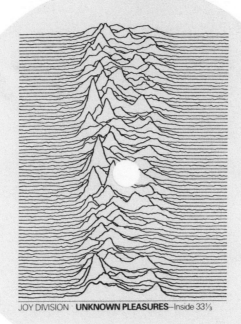

# STUFF THE SUPERSTARS
# FUNHOUSE AT THE MAYFLOWER CLUB
## SAT 28TH JULY

DOORS OPEN 1.30 p.m. BANDS FROM 2.00 Till LATE.

IN ORDER OF APPEARANCE......

## HAMSTERS
## ELTI FITS
## ARMED FORCE
## FRANTIC ELEVATORS
## JOY DIVISION

## LUDUS
## THE LIGGERS
## THE FALL
## THE DISTRACTIONS
## JON THE POSTMAN
PSYCHEDELIC R'n'R 5 SKINNERS

TICKETS AVAILABLE FROM:- DISCOUNT RECORDS (Underground Market)
PICCADILLY RECORDS (Piccadilly Plaza)

TICKETS £1.50      TICKETS £1.50      TICKETS £1.50

STUFF THE SUPERSTARS SPECIAL FESTIVAL......SATURDAY 28th JULY
FUNHOUSE AT THE MAYFLOWER CLUB.............
BAR 1.30 - 3.00 & 5.30 til LATE. FOOD AVAILABLE ALL DAY......
RECORDS, BADGES, FANZINES, etc, ON SALE (CHEAP!!!)...........
ALL PROFITS AFTER EXPENSES WILL BE SPLIT EQUALLY BETWEEN THE BANDS.

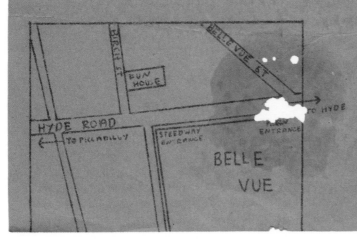

BUSES:-
From Piccadilly: 125,126,160,
204,205,206,207,208,209,210,
211,212,233,234,235.
From Cheetham/Clayton: 53.
From Old Trafford/Moss Side:53.
From Denton & Hyde 125,207-212
From Droylsden: 169, 170.
From Didsbury & Burnage:169,170

GIG GUIDE

JULY 10th : RARE DEVICE,PROPERTY OF...,EMPEROR ROATH AND THE GALACTIC EMPIRE.
         BAND ON THE WALL.

JULY 11th : ROCK AGAINST RACISM. THE FACTORY. - NAUGHTY BOYS.

JULY 12th : NEON,VIBRANT THIGH. THE FACTORY.

JULY 13TH : FRIDAY  : JOY DIVISION. THE FACTORY.

JULY 17th : TUESDAY : DUFFO. THE FACTORY.

JULY 17th : TUESDAY : CRISPY AMBULANCE,THE ENIGMA,THE LIGGERS. BAND ON THE WALL.

JULY 18th : WEDNES  : THE ACCELERATORS,NAUGHTY LUMPS. THE FACTORY.

JULY 19th : THURSDAY: LORD CASS,BLACKA BULLET(SOUND SYSTEMS). THE FACTORY.

JULY 20th : FRIDAY  : THE FALL,ECHO AND THE BUNNYMEN. THE FACTORY.

JULY 20th : FRIDAY  : TRADITION. MAYFLOWER CLUB.

JULY 21st : SATURDAY: ADAM AND THE ANTS. THE FACTORY.

JULY 25th : BITING TONGUES. THE FACTORY.

JULY 24th : UNITS,THE HOAX,THE VIBRANT THIGH. BAND ON THE WALL.

JULY 26th : SUGAR MISFIT. THE FACTORY.

JULY 27th : U.K. SUBS. THE FACTORY.

JULY 28th : STUFF THE SUPERSTARS SPECIAL FESTIVAL - THE HAMSTERS,ELTI FITS,
         ARMED FORCE, FRANTIC ELEVATORS, JOY DIVISION,LUDUS, THE LIGGERS,
         THE FALL, THE DISTRACTIONS, JON THE POSTMANS PSYCHEDELIC R'n'R
         5 SKINNERS. FUNHOUSE at the MAYFLOWER CLUB.

JULY 30th : MANCHESTER MUSICIANS COLLECTIVE MEETING. NORTH WEST ARTS.(52 King St).

JULY 31st : FEATURES,PROPERTY OF... . BAND ON THE WALL.

AUGUST 2nd: BLACKA BULLET SOUND SYSTEM. THE FACTORY.

AUGUST 4th: THE PRETENDERS. THE FACTORY.

AUGUST 4th: V2. FUNHOUSE (at the MAYFLOWER).

AUGUST 6th: SLAUGHTER AND THE DOGS. THE FACTORY.

AUGUST 7th: GROW UP,STEVE MYRO AND THE EYES,IQ ZERO. BAND ON THE WALL.

AUGUST 10th: THE SPECIALS,PRIVATE SECTOR. THE FUNHOUSE.

AUGUST 11th: THE SLITS. THE FACTORY.


LATE ADDITIONS...LATE ADDITIONS...LATE ADDITIONS...

JULY 26th : THE ZONES. FUNHOUSE.

JULY 14th : ARMED FORCE. R.A.R. ROCHDALE TECH.


NEWS Alan Wise is handing over managership of the Factory to Gwyn Roberts.

The FUNHOUSE, a new venue is opening at what used to be the Mayflower Club.
Myself (Andy Zero) and Rob Crane will be promoting the groups. Watch press
for details.

051-236 8301
9 Mathew Street
Liverpool 2

|  |  |  | members | guests |
|---|---|---|---|---|
| Thur 29 Nov | TOURS |  | 75p | £1 |
| Fri 30 Nov | SIMPLE MINDS + The Portraits |  | £1-10 | £1-60 |
| Sat 1 Dec | THE POP GROUP + The Delta Five | Evg Only | £1-35 | £1-75 |
| Thur 6 Dec | JUNK ART + guests |  | free | 50p |
| Fri 7 Dec | THE MODETTES + Wah Heat |  | £1-10 | £1-60 |
| Sat 8 Dec | JOY DIVISION + Section 25 | Mat 5 pm | £1-10 | £1-35 |
|  |  | Evg 8.30 | £1-35 | £1-75 |
| Thur 13 Dec | STEEL PULSE |  | £1-50 | £2-00 |
| Fri 14 Dec | Jak Jones presents The PIRATES + The Nice Men |  | £1-25 | £1-75 |
| Sat 15 Dec | EDDIE & THE HOT RODS + guests | Evg Only | £1-35 | £1-75 |
| Mon 17 Dec | THE DAMNED + The Victims |  | £1-50 | £2-00 |
| Wed 19 Dec | THE BEAT + God's Toys |  | £1-25 | £1-75 |
| Thur 20 Dec | Open Eye Christmas Party with THOSE NAUGHTY LUMPS / THE MODERATES / ROY WHITE & STEVE TORCH |  | 75p adv £1 door |  |
| Fri 21 Dec | Lesley Palmer presents a Christmas Reggae Party with THE MIGHTY VHYBES + I SOCIETY + THE PEOPLE'S SOUND SYSTEM |  | £1 | £1-50 |
| Sat 22 Dec | ERIC'S CHRISTMAS PARTY with THE TEARDROP EXPLODES + ECHO & THE BUNNYMEN |  |  |  |
|  |  | Mat 5 pm | £1-10 | £1-35 |
|  |  | Evg 8.30 | £1-50 | £2-00 |
| Thur 27 Dec | Skeleton Records present THE ZORKIE TWINS / JUNK ART / ATTEMPTED MUSTACHE / THE POSERS / TIM BYERS |  | 75p | £1 |
| Fri 28 Dec | A TRIBUTE TO WINSTON featuring members of ORCHESTRAL MANOEUVRES IN THE DARK and DALEK I |  | £1-10 | £1-60 |
| Sat 29 Dec | A Rhythm & Blues Special with LEW LEWIS and BAD MANNERS | Evg Only | £1-35 | £1-75 |

Hours of Opening: 8.30-2am (Matinee Saturdays 5-7.30pm) We are open between mid-day and 2 pm daily except Sunday for badges, posters, T-shirts and membership enquiries.
SHOW TIMES: On all shows except Saturday the support will be on stage at 9.30 and the main band at approx 10.45. On Saturdays the main band will be onstage at 10 pm and the support group will play at approx 11.30 pm. The door admission price will be reduced when the main band have finished their set.
MEMBERSHIP OF ERIC'S is £1-10 yearly. A member is entitled to sign in two guests, and to benefit from reduced admission prices. Membership application forms are available from the Club. Call us on our 24-hour answering service **051-236 8301** for further information.

APPENDIX TWO

# AMES
## RECORDS + TAPES

FROM BAUHAUS TO BEETHOVEN AND BACK. LARGE SELECTION OF IMPORTS, INDEPENDENTS, 12 inch. COMPACT DISCS, VIDEOS.

AMES RECORDS + TAPES
20 DEANERY WAY
STOCKPORT.

# RARE
## RECORDS

**CASSETTES**
SINGLES
**ALBUMS**

Rare Records Ltd., 13 Bank Square,
Wilmslow, Cheshire SK9 1AN
Tel: Wilmslow (0625) 522017

# Harlequin●

- BOOKS, POSTERS, PHOTOS......
- ROCK, MOVIE, T.V. STARS......
- STATE INTERESTS......

# GIANT ILLUST. CATALOGUE
☐ SEND 20p + S.A.E. to HARLEQUIN,
68 ST. PETERSGATE, STOCKPORT

The Calm Before The Storm
By
Mick Middles

## JOY DIVISION.

Through geographical good fortune I became the first person to interview Joy Division
for the national music press. Typically, the London editorial couldn't see value in
affording space to an unproven northern band and the interview was savagely cut into
a rather messy and directionless affair. It was only upon accidentally stumbling across
the original interview tape, some five years later, that I realised just how revealing
the entire piece would be if revitalised.
To be fair, the interview was conducted at a time when the bands promise was only in
its embryonic stages and few people could forsee these four naive hopefuls swiftly
evolving into the most important music force of the last decade. The very idea would
have seemed preposterous. Their previous dates at the Band On The Wall and The Factory
had shown promise but there was little evidence of anything other than a powerful but
limited stab at sub-Banshee rocky pretension. Something drew me towards the interview
situation though, maybe nothing more than the constant pleadings of their new manager,
Rob Gretton whose previous claims to fame were as nothing more than Rafters D.J. and
the creator of the truly awful Slaughter And The Dogs fanzine 'Manchester Reigns'. The
latter being in thuggish reference to Gretton's Saturday afternoon activities as a
basher of the 'non Blues' at Maine Road.
I remember the approach to the interview with detailed clarity. Huddled in the corner
of one of Tony Davidson's practice rooms, the band appeared even more nervous than
I. Terrified of ruining their doomy image and basking in a typically naive sense of the
over-dramatic, they wouldn't allow themselves to open up. I decided that a trip to the
local pub would help that ice to vanish. Dutifully, they trooped into The Gaythorne.
A pub, ironically situated just a few yards from what would eventually become The
Hacienda.
IAN CURTIS. "You want a brief history? er..It was January '77 we got together and we
first played in May at The Electric Circus with The Buzzcocks and Penetration."
BARNEY. "Y'see what happened was that me and Hooky..the bass player. We started off..,
well I had a guitar, he got a bass and we just started messing about in the back room
and then we advertised in Virgin for a singer. Ian answered it. We got that far but
we had a job after that getting a drummer. We had about five drummers."
ROB. "One of them was that er big mouth..Steve out of V.2. He would give out incredible
stories of tours of America.."
BARNEY. "Well, the night before we played at The Electric Circus..we got a drummer. All
the songs that we'd wrote we'd not wrote with a drummer so it was a bit odd when we
played them.
STEVE. "That last night at the Electric Circus was a complete fuck up though. We thought
we were playing on the Saturday so we all rolled up and they said "No, your on tommorrow".
So we came back and.."
IAN. "There was just loads of bands wandering about and about three different running
orders knocking about. Everyone had a different list, no one knew what was going on. It
was Richard Boon (Buzzcocks manager, nowadays to be seen esconsed in the ivory towers
of Rough Trade) who put us on. We've had alot of dealings with him. He used to come
down to a lot of rehearsals when we used to practise in Salford with no drummer and I
think he wanted to manage us."
ROB. "It was him who called you Stiff Kittens wasn't it? They upset him because they
chose Warsaw. He wanted to take them under his wing."
Do you write your songs collectively? Who comes up with the ideas?
IAN. "It varies, doesn't it? We usually start with a drum riff and put a bass on top of
that.."
BARNEY. "Then Ian adds lyrics. He's got a book full of them and he picks something
suitable to the tune. He writes all the time anyway, don't you?"
IAN. "Yeah well take 'Leaders Of Men'. Some of the lyrics to that are two or three
years old. I just add bits..Keep finding bits to use."
What are they about?
IAN. "Various things really. I tend not to write about anything in particular. If some-
thing strikes me. I tend to write very subconciously sometimes. Like, well I don't know
what they are about. It depends really..er..."
Well, for instance songs on your E.P. What is 'Leaders Of Men' about?
IAN. "Pretty obvious song that, pretty obvious really..I like to leave it open to
interpretation. It is pointless writing about specific things then it's going to be
dated. The E.P. is a year old now..really. It was recorded last year."
Did that get a lot of radio play?

**5**

ROB. "Peely played it a lot. It has been played on Radio Manchester's rock show. They said that we had been signed to R.C.A. Well, ha, that's a complicated story which we'd rather you didn't mention just know but, before I became the manager they went into the studio and recorded an album.which, they had signed a contract, stupidly, to this production house and it was going to be leased to R.C.A."

STEVE. "Well originally they were going to lease it all over the world..they said."

ROB. "When I became manager they had already recorded this. The blokes from the company were real idiots well, the band were idiots for signing it and,, well, it was a big rip off anyway so we are still in the process of extracating ourselves from this."

STEVE."Originally it was just a single and we said no. We thought we couldn't sign for three years for just one single...Then this guy comes back from America and says "We want you to do an album" and we thought, 'Great..We'll be stars'. Being a bit naive we signed it' How did you get in with Rough Trade then?

ROB. "Well Rough Trade always wanted to re-issue the single anyway so I made sure they did it on a twelve inch. It's just a ploy really, because we are involved in getting out of this stupid contract we needed to keep the name in the public eye. So a re-issue was the perfect way of doing this. This is why I asked you to do this."

Have you anything else lined up then?

ROB. "Yeah, we have but..ha..again I'd rather you didn't mention it . We've got a single coming out.Two new songs for a thing that Roger Eagles and Tony Wilson are starting called Factory Records with four bands. Joy Division, Caberet Voltaire, Durrutti Column and John Dowie. We've already recorded it but it's only half legal at present.We'd better change the subject..It seems like a good opportunity for us..I think.We wont play London untill the single is out."

BARNEY."Look, Ian, just give me a quick squirt of your sauce..This pie is dry."

When everybody says Joy Division then pin you with this nazi thing...

IAN. "Why? Because we were called Warsaw? It was just a nothing name.Pretty bleak. I got Joy Division out of a 1984 type book. It' ironic because most of the music is doomy. When we called ourselves Joy Division everybody thought we were a Salvation Army band. Or a bunch of studs. Everybody hated it so we thought we'd keep it."

ROB. "I think people are very naive. They jump to conclusions. When you wrote that review, which I couldn't understand, you mentioned that we used this nazi chic. Why?"

"ALL DRESSED UP IN UNIFORMS SO FINE, WITH MEASURED STEPS THEY WALKED IN LINES". (From 'Walked in Lines)

ROB. "Yeah but compared to Jimmy Pursey who is an out and out racist.."

Why?

IAN. "Yeah, you don't think so. That just proves our point. Everyone forgets that Jimmy Pursey, when they first started out they said "We hate The Sex Pistols, We are for the real kids who go Paki bashing down the Eastend."

ROB. "He pretends it's all coincidence that all these British Movement skins are following him about but he made that happen. Fair enough he can change his mind and, well I don't like the guy."

IAN. "All this Rock Against Racism shit is really patronising. I hate it."

STEVE. "It's like saying the blacks can't help themselves so we are helping them."

So you wouldn't play for Rock Against Racism?

ROB. "Yeah, we did one last week."

Just for the money?

ROB. "No..no We are against racism it's just the attitude that people like Jimmy Pursey take that annoys us..Anyway, you avoided the question. Why nazi chic?"

The way that you dress.

IAN."Huh, what."

ROB. "Look, I'm not supposed to say this but their image is supposed to be dark and doomy. Why is that considered to be nazi?"

Or clean cut. The Hitler youth look.

IAN. "No, that can't be..can it?"

ROB. "Onstage they may appear aloof. They don't pamper the audience. I don't see why you have to pamper to an audience anyway."

Because they have payed to see you, maybe. Because you owe them a pounds worth of entertainment.

HOOKEY. (Previously adopting the silent and moody approach)."That's a really good point. We should think about it."

The band and Rob engage in mock deep thought.

Everybody in unison. "NAA, FUCK THEM".

copyright.Mick Middles. 78.

ARTWORK, FANZINES, BOOKS, LETTERS                    231

One year old today- The Factory birthday
party -friday may 11th. A full moon.
   Arriving late, finally, missing A CERTAIN
RATIO, a pity-a good single- until next time
Missing most of, ORCHESTRAL MANOUVRES IN THE
DARK. Entering the club, they are onstage,
their prescence is psychedelic extreme,
visual- blue tinged a fluorescent strip
stands verticle stage left, the stage is
bathed with constant light. The guitarist
stands stage right, he also sings; he
doesnt move about much. The keyboards
player stands stage left- behind his
instruments, sometimes he plays with one
hand while hopping up and down. The reel to
reel tape recorder stands at the back, stage
centre, it always looks the same....recorded
on the tape is a bass line, electronic howls
and screeches, and whines. The bass line is
continual bubbling metronomic disco.
Ambience like Kraftwerk. Keyboards playing
light catchy melody- 'Electricity', their
single- intense pop, commercial sound as in
Tubeway Army, remains in memory. Layered
electronic swirling music fills the room.
Good P.A., clear sound. The 'band' is worth
seeing.
   A short break: you can talk to your
friends, get yourself a drink, dance to the
disco, sit with yourself (waiting for the
band), have oral sex with a partner. You
have a choice.
   JOHN DOWIE -didn't like him last time i
saw him- Tonight he's playing with a band,
a definite improvement. 'British Tourist',
his"I hate the Dutch" tirade, takes on a new
significance as i realise it's a pisstake. I
quite enjoy myself. He performs his last two
songs alone and receives a fair applause for
his entertainment.
   JOY DIVISION, finally on stage..........
reviewed them two issues ago, tonight i just
enjoy myself. A brilliant start, i dance and
i'm not alone. Rhythm hypnotic, intense.
Vocalist Ian Curtis contorts and jerks, his
stark figure the key point of their presence
After two years gigging they play consistent
good music. Two years building a following
in Manchester. So i'm familiar with the
songs, though not their titles. Dancing i'm
pissed and enjoying it. They play an encore
and are good.
   The Factory is one year old, so what, it's
a full moon, we go home.
                               Andy Zero
THE BUZZCOCKS : JOHN COOPER CLARKE
The Factory.
Not a proper gig-being filmed for Granada T.V.
Word of mouth advertising.£1 in. The stage
looks like a television studio - a special
backdrop, special lighting.
   JOHN COOPER CLARKE is on first. Prancing
and posing he recites various poems from his
book. I'm talking so only remember 'Twat'

which raises a few laughs. Two men wearing
large white t.v. cameras like parrots on th
shoulders lurch about within a few feet of
and he does his best to avoid and ignore the
He gets a few laughs and some applause thou
it will hardly be seen as an audience respo
of our time.
*Who exactly is this audience, very few
Factory regulars, large contingents of the
'in' crowd (in what??), are these people her
because they actually like The Buzzcocks?
Because it's THE BUZZCOCKS at the factory f
a quid?? Because(is that really you on TV)
be seen to be hip- poseurs anonymous annual
convention??? Or what.*
   Granada televisions Tony Wilson informs
that The Buzzcocks will be on shortly. 5 mi
later they appear on stage. The cameras hav
to be set and adjusted- this takes time you
understand. The Buzzcocks take up a blues j
and it proves to be the most spontaneous
creativity of the night
   The set is predictable- 'The Best of The
Buzzcocks'/'The Buzzcocks Greatest Hits Vol
Opening with 'I don't mind', through 'Ever
Fallen In Love'.....'What Do I Get'...The fi
half of the set is dissapointing, where is
energy.
   Each time i see The Buzzcocks they're mo
polished, more precise, tighter. Tonight is
exception. Their clothes are expensive, not
flash, tasteful.
   We are on television. Safe for T.V. The
Buzzcocksplaying sanitised rock and roll fo
the masses. Sterilised Buzzcocksplaying to
order- strictly to rule- rehearsed tight- n
invention and little feel.
   I'd forgotton just how good The Buzzcock
are. The songs they play are classics.
Immaculate light machine music. They also
are dance music for mind and body.
   They warm up towards the end, 'Autonomy'
and 'E.S.P.' were good, sharp and clean. The
contain a spark that was patently missing
earlier. Pete Shelly's vocals over dynamica
surging guitar is ecstatic. Obvious fans dan
energetically in a small group.
   Few people actually strain themselves fo
an encore but we get one in anycase. Filmed
for posterity and money.
The television crew provide us with some
amusing moments. Getting on Steve Diggles
nerves,as a camera approaches within two
feet of his face,he bends forward and peers
into it, the camera beat a hasty retreat.
Filming John Maher the camera leans over hi
shoulder about three inches away.
   Tonight is television but i danced to
rock and Roll. Though the feelinghas it that
the Buzzcocks are fucked they still cut it
the stage. Manchester is watching.
                               Andy Zero

APPENDIX TWO

APPENDIX TWO

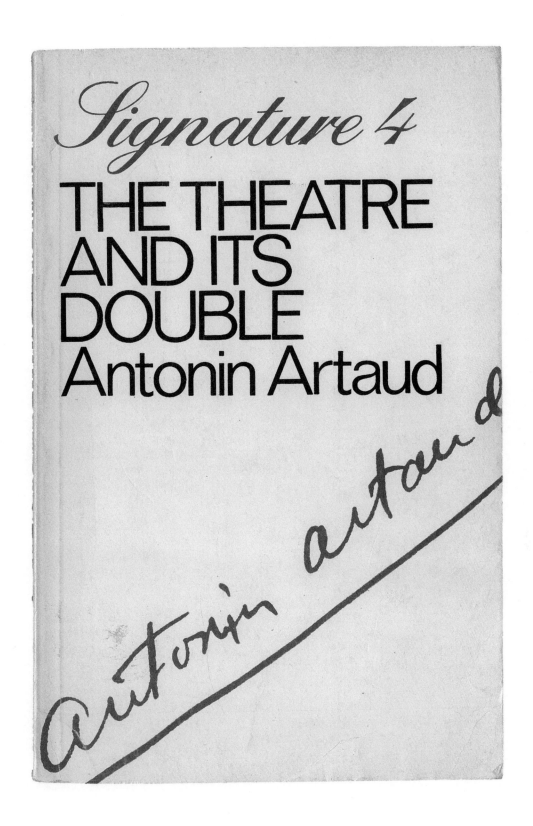

Adrian Henri

# Environments
# and Happenings

with 150 illustrations
30 in colour

The World of Art
Library
NEW DIRECTIONS
Thames and
Hudson

238                                        APPENDIX TWO

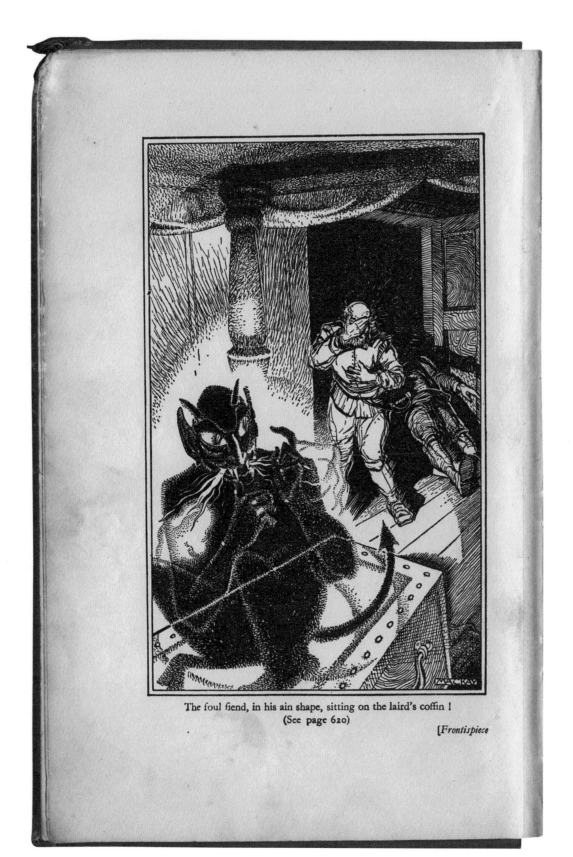

The foul fiend, in his ain shape, sitting on the laird's coffin !
(See page 620)

[Frontispiece

APPENDIX TWO

# A CENTURY
# OF THRILLERS

## FROM POE TO ARLEN

*With a Foreword by*
**JAMES AGATE**

*FIFTH IMPRESSION*

LONDON
DAILY EXPRESS PUBLICATIONS
1934

OSCAR WILDE
*From the painting by Toulouse-Lautrec, 1895.*

APPENDIX TWO

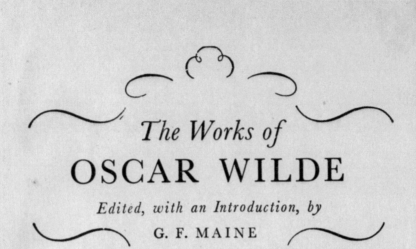

*The Works of*

# OSCAR WILDE

*Edited, with an Introduction, by*

G. F. MAINE

COLLINS
LONDON AND GLASGOW

RIMBAUD

# A SEASON IN HELL
# THE ILLUMINATIONS

A new translation by
Enid Rhodes Peschel

OXFORD
PAPERBACKS

The
Auto-
Biography
&
Sex Life
of

ANDY

WARHOL

by

John

Wilcock

with a cast

of thousands

five dollars

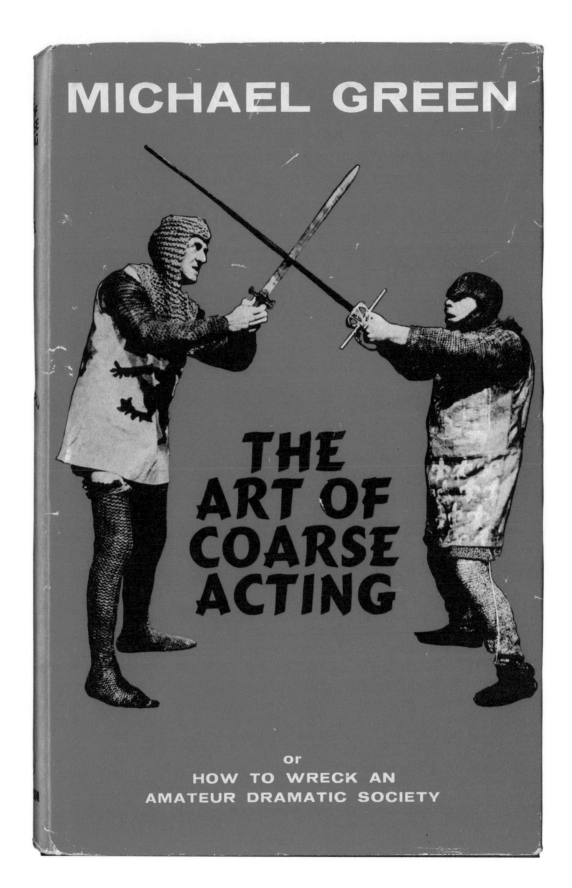

THE KING'S SCHOOL,
MACCLESFIELD.

*History* Prize.

Form *L5M*

Awarded to:

*I. K. Curtis*

on

A. H. COOPER,
Headmaster.

**ALDOUS HUXLEY**

BRAVE NEW WORLD

Panther 0 586 04434 5

Dawn Ades
**Dada and Surrealism**
64 pages in colour

APPENDIX TWO

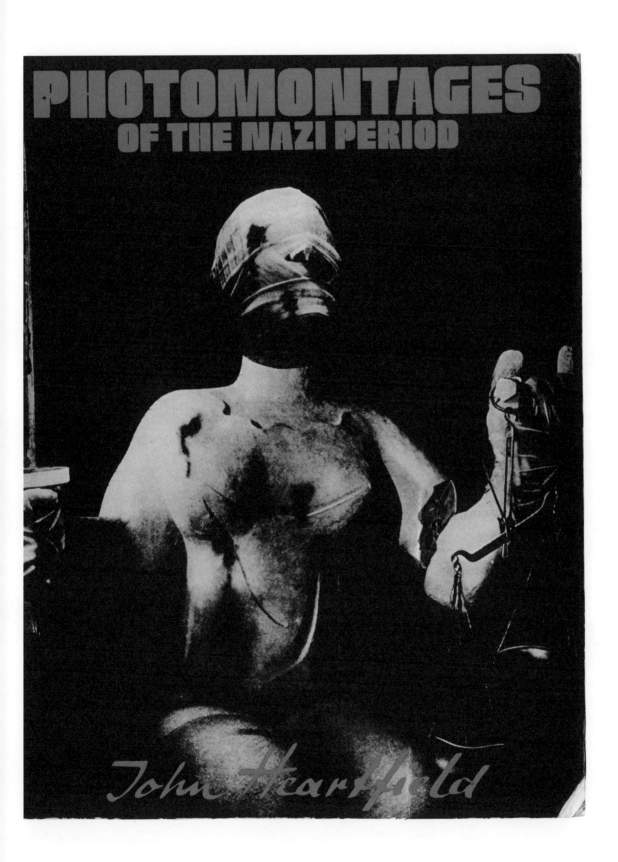

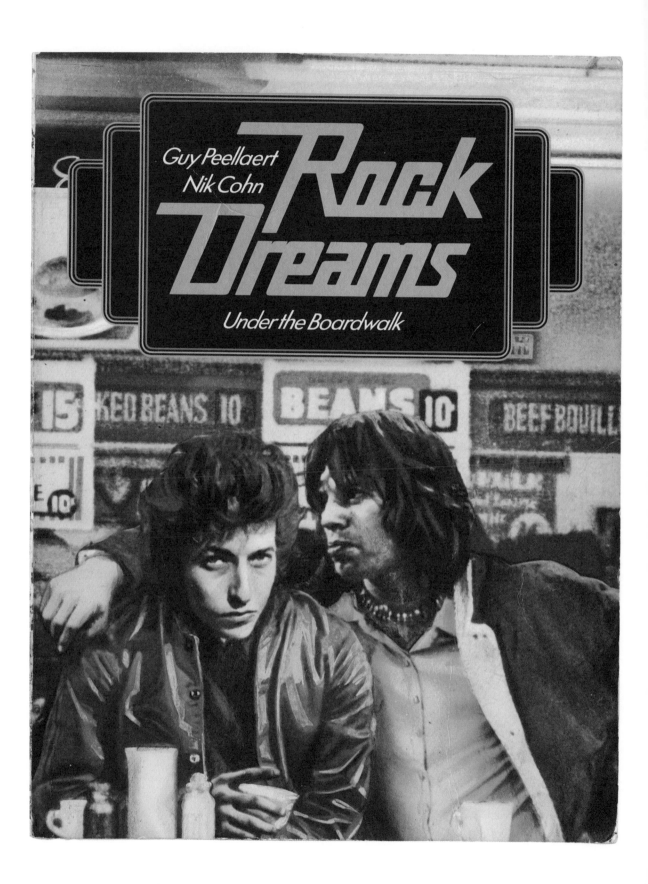

# POEMS

## SELECTED

## Thom Gunn & Ted Hughes

**FABER**

FABER paper covered EDITIONS

PENGUIN CLASSICS

NIETZSCHE
THUS SPOKE ZARATHUSTRA

Ian Curtis,
77, Barton Sreet,
Macclesfield,
Cheshire

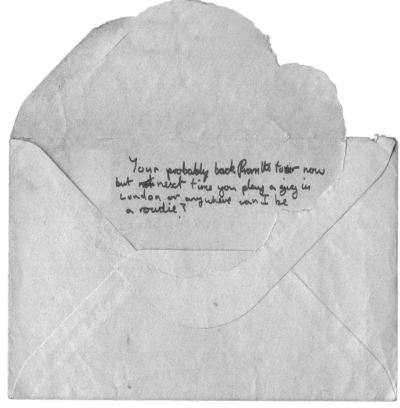

Your probably back from the tour now
but next time you play a gig in
London or anywhere can I be
a roudie?

Rex,
▬▬ ▬
Chorley,
Lancs,
▬▬▬

Dear Ian,
its Rex thanks
for getting me in on Friday it was
great! (not just saying it to crawl)
I'll ring you soon or you ring
me (chorley ▬▬▬▬▬▬). Also
when's your birthday I've gott an
ace present for you. Is there any
slightchance at all you can get
"Ideal for Living" as I want it
desprately 7" & 12". The paper
I'm writing on is a souvineer
from Friday for (great wow gdy)
Next time I write to you can
I send you a tape and on can
you put some v. early, early,
medium, present stuff on it
(please) can you send some more
unknown pleasure 5 badge cos I
ve only 1 left
        See- Ya soon Rex Gorgeous
Here

SUN. 28th

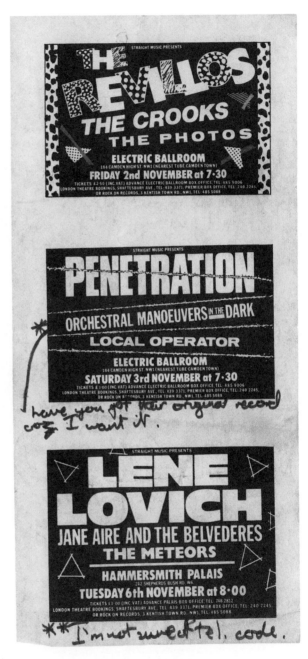

have you got their original record
cos I want it.

** I'm not sure of tel. code.

Dear Joy Division,

I write you stupidly but it's a need.
I write you to say —
Your sound is a mother voice.
I know (I find) it's useless to write to
somebody how wonderful he is but it's
a need; it's the first time I write so and also
probably the last time.

Sensible People are too rare in the mondial area to ignore them.
What you are doing bless me like "Hiroshima mon amour"
from Alain Remais or like the songs sung by Edith PIAF.

People Too many people are vulgar. I feel dispirit
I love 20 persons and I have the envy to kill the others.
But if people are so vulgar, they are too vulgar to be considered.
They are unable too love. They are unable to suffer. They
are unable to cry. They seems unable to live.
DON'T DIE, please.

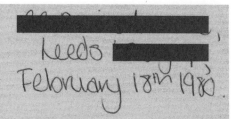

Leeds ████

February 18th 1980.

Dear Ian,

I heard Joy Division play
in Leeds last year and bought
"Unknown Pleasures" soon after. Since
when I have been trying to get
hold of a Joy Division badge, however
there doesn't seem to be such a thing
on sale in Leeds. I wondered if you
could send me details about where
I could get one from. I have enclosed
a stamped adressed envelope.

Will you be playing in Leeds
soon?

Love

████

x x x

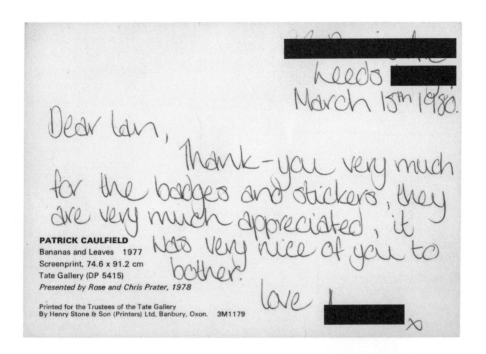

Leeds ████
March 15th 1980.

Dear Ian,

Thank-you very much for the badges and stickers, they are very much appreciated, it was very nice of you to bother.

love ████ x

PATRICK CAULFIELD
Bananas and Leaves 1977
Screenprint, 74.6 x 91.2 cm
Tate Gallery (DP 5415)
*Presented by Rose and Chris Prater, 1978*

Printed for the Trustees of the Tate Gallery
By Henry Stone & Son (Printers) Ltd, Banbury, Oxon. 3M1179

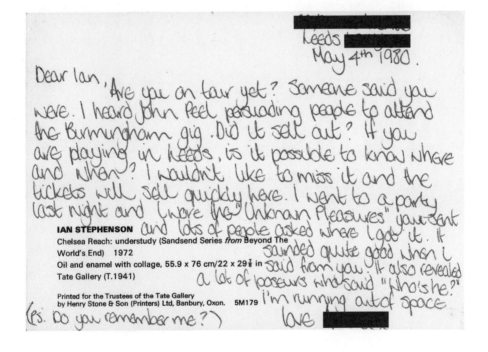

Leeds ████
May 4th 1980.

Dear Ian, Are you on tour yet? Someone said you were. I heard John Peel persuading people to attend the Birmingham gig. Did it sell out? If you are playing in Leeds, is it possible to know where and when? I wouldn't like to miss it and the tickets will sell quickly here. I went to a party last night and I wore the "Unknown Pleasures" you sent and lots of people asked where I got it. It sounded quite good when I said from you. It also revealed a lot of poseurs who said "Who's he?" I'm running out of space

(P.s. Do you remember me?)

love ████

IAN STEPHENSON
Chelsea Reach: understudy (Sandsend Series *from* Beyond The World's End) 1972
Oil and enamel with collage, 55.9 x 76 cm/22 x 29⅞ in
Tate Gallery (T.1941)

Printed for the Trustees of the Tate Gallery
by Henry Stone & Son (Printers) Ltd, Banbury, Oxon. 5M179

YEOVIL
SOMERSET

Dear Ian,

I'll try not to take up too much of your time as you must be pretty busy now with the day to day running of your group.

I will come straight to the point, the music of the Joy Division means most to me now, I paint and draw a lot and play tapes and records while I am working. I like Debussy, Satie piano music, Public Image Limited, Ultravox, loads of other things but Joy Division have pretty well enraptured me for the past two months. It is so good to dance too as well as to reflect on, Peter Hook's bass lines, your voice, that soaring guitar and precision drumming just go round my head from day to day. I would like to read your lyrics, I realise the words to the whole album is asking a bit much so I wonder if you could just space me a moment of time and send me the words to the tracks that I find most haunting of all, 'Shadowplay' and 'Transmission'.

I feel a bit of a shit writing to you and asking this of you as this seems to be part of the old system of things, the 'fans' draining the groups, all take and no give. If you have time to oblige, I shall send you a drawing or something in return. I guess the demands on you must be getting greater, I wish you luck with everything that you want with Joy Division.

　　　　　Yours sincerely
　　　　　Steve Batty.

P.S. 'Transmission' sold out first day it arrived in Yeovil.
P.P.S. I hope the bloke I phoned to find Factory's address has
　　　　got rid of his cold!

Thursday10th. April.

Dear Ian.

It was very kind of you to drop me a line and send the words of
"Shadowplay"and"Transmission"and the badges.May I thank you
very much and also apologise for having not replied sooner;I
have been busy lately,amongst other things with the enclosed
cower illustrations for you.As far as being interpretations of
the songs goes,they are pretty much in the wind as I havent hea
rd "Atmosphere"or"Dead Souls",so Ive gone on the feelings im the
titles.The local record shop say they may be getting in a few
copies of"Licht und Blindheit"I hope they do,it sounds very
interesting from what Ive heard,and what you said in your letter
;are there any plans to release it im larger numbers on Factory?
I expect by now you are finishing off the album,I hope everything
is going well,and that your short tour of the Continent went O.K.
It is good that you have some say in the total direction of the
band,management wise;this is the thing with something as parochial
as Factory,your success is verification that the state of music is
capable of change.In many ways I am glad that you are not doing
Big tours,I can imagine it must be a real fuck up to have to go
on stage every day and I know that you are about to do nothing else
but give your all into performance.The world of constant rock n roll
or whatever is an inward looking festering scab,a childish demand.
Groups like yours have gone a long way to change things for the
better.
Even if yourgroup and your sound had happened without the changes,
if,say"Punk"hadnt happened but there still came along Joy Division
you still would have been worth listening too.Your sounds ,the vocals
,the lyrics are strength enough,the way these sounds are marketed,
thought about,communicated,is the bonus.Im sure you are recognised
for this today and will be recognised im the future.The fact you
arent plastered over all the music papers and on the radio all the
time is to your credit.I expect that sounds all calculated;the
beauty of your music and everything is its divergence from calcu
lation,like the grey areas your songs evoke.There is such a lot im
the rythm and vocals and the lyrics that defies description(in the
same way that the songs are feelings from some twilight zone of
mature,beyond description,pure feeling).I think a lot of rock music
is like that anyway,I remember seeing a play on T.V.im which they
explained rock as a by pass of reason straight into feeling,up
until now the only feelings expressed using electric instruments
have almost totally been geard d up to some kind of sexual/sexist
display,which is fair enough seeing that sex is one of the nearest
basic feelings,but Idd never until I first heard and saw Joy
Division on "Something Else"witnessed an expression from the heart
quite like your performance and the sheer fearful sound.YOu see,Ive
tried to describe all that and look how long its taken,whereas the
feeling for all that and the knowledge and the impulse take up so lit
tle space("No language just sound is all we need know").
I know when the local groups here get together the sound of frantic
tuning up at the beginning of e ach set is a very exciting .There are
about four or five bands here,The Mob have got the furthest,theyve
been associated with the Here & Now/Wierd Tales axis and have their
own single out next Wednesday.Its still very difficult to run events
down here ,nowhere in Yeowil will allow the dreaded "Punk Rock"and
the village halls im the satellite places are becoming less available
due to the violence that you get at the concerts by the bikers.But
im amongst The Wurzels records and the heavy metal bands there is
some taste.why,I even borrowe d your early "Ideal For Living"E.P.off
one of the punks .I really like "Leaders Of Men".
Well looks like its time to go,I hope you like the drawings,they are
the nearest I could get to giving back something of the feelings im
your music.Write and let me know how things are going ,perhaps if
you have got a minute you could write out some more lyrics to some
of the songs.Do you think Sordide Sentimentale will have many copies
of"Licht und Bli ndheit"left.If so could you forward their address.
I would be very grateful.Thanks once again for the letter.
Hope to hear from you soon.

yours sincerely

Steve Batty.

JOY DIVISION     DEAD SOULS

JOY DIVISION                    ATMOSPHERE

██████████████
███████████

Leyland
██████████
Lancs.

Dear Ian,

I hope you and the band
enjoyed the warehouse! It was a
pity about the equipment but what
you did play was good.

I hope you did'nt take my
brother seriously, nobody does. He's
a tit who thinks he's hyperactive,
he's been like that since he was a
child when my sister used to wobble
his head!

You never met my friend, Christine.
That's because she was'nt there. I
ran away from home with her. We
were bored so we caught a train
to Blackpool at 7·00 o'clock on a
Wednesday night. It was fun!
Afterwards we had to see a priest
and everyone thought we were
phycopaths (which I can't spell)

Ian said you like Cabaret
Voltaire (The Cabs - if you want to
use hip jargon!) Have you heard the

APPENDIX TWO

LP 'Mix-up' I like "Expect Nothing" +
"4th Shot"

I am going to a jumble sale today,
I've got to get my brother a big
collared flowery shirt. I hope I find
some bargains!

Speaking of my brother, guess what
he got me for christmas? A Blue Stratos
gift set. I asked for Metal Box - which
he got me, then changed his mind.

Sorry if I'm boring I've just
woken up! I am going to see The Fall
at Erics next Saturday. I hope they
are better than they were at Blackpool!

Anyway must go to the jumble
sale and get myself a new outfit!

P.S my mother just nagged at me!
yesterday she nagged 12 times.

# ACKNOWLEDGEMENTS

FROM JON SAVAGE

Thanks to Deborah Curtis, David Brown, Lesley Gilbert, Rebecca Boulton, Andy Robinson, Jon Wozencroft, Michael Butterworth, Mark Reeder and the four members of Joy Division: Ian Curtis, Bernard Sumner, Peter Hook and Stephen Morris.

FROM DEBORAH CURTIS

Thanks to my parents Bob and Audrey, my partner David and to Jon Savage for his friendship and guidance.

INDIVIDUAL PERMISSIONS:

Photo p. vi © Mark Reeder
Interview and artwork pp. 229–31 © Mick Middles
Letter pp. 260–61 © Rex Sargeant
Letters and artwork pp. 266–69 © Steve Batty
Letters pp. 262–63, 264–65, 270–71 © the individual authors

BOOK COVER PERMISSIONS:

*The Theatre and its Double*, reproduced with permission from Alma Books Ltd; *Environments and Happenings*, reproduced with permission from Thames & Hudson Ltd; *A Season in Hell: The Illuminations*, translated by Peschel (1974) cover: by permission of Oxford University Press, USA; *The Auto-Biography and Sex Life of Andy Warhol*, reproduced with permissions from John Wilcock; *The Art of Coarse Acting*, courtesy of Hutchinson/Random House Group; *Brave New World*, courtesy of Panther/HarperCollins Publishers Ltd; *A Clockwork Orange*: reproduced with permission from Penguin Books Ltd; *Dada and Surrealism*: reproduced with permission from Thames & Hudson Ltd; *The Idiot*, reproduced with permission from Penguin Books Ltd; *Nausea*, reproduced with permission from Penguin Books Ltd; *Photomontages of the Nazi Period*, courtesy of Gordon Fraser Gallery in association with Universe Books; *Rock Dreams: Under the Boardwalk*, courtesy of Pan Macmillan; *Steppenwolf*, reproduced with permission from Penguin Books Ltd; *Thus Spoke Zarathustra*, reproduced with permission from Penguin Books Ltd; *Twilight of the Idols of the Anti-Christ*, reproduced with permission from Penguin Books Ltd; *White Subway*, Book Cover Design: Jim Pennington from a photograph by Max Blagg, NYC, 1971, courtesy of Aloes Books.

*Every effort has been made to trace or contact all copyright holders. The publishers would be pleased to rectify at the earliest opportunity any errors or omissions brought to their notice.*